THE BEST MOVIE THEMES EVER

Winter '20

ISBN 978-1-4950-7332-8

7777 W. BLUEMOUND RD. P.O. BOX 13819 MILWAUKEE, WI 53213

Visit Hal Leonard Online at
www.halleonard.com

AIRPORT LOVE THEME
(Winds of Chance)
from AIRPORT

Words by PAUL FRANCIS WEBSTER
Music by ALFRED NEWMAN

Slowly, with expression

mf

With pedal

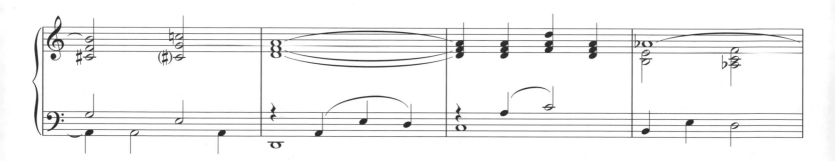

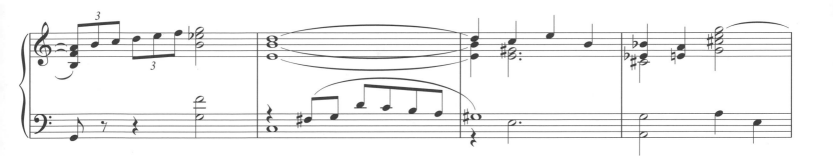

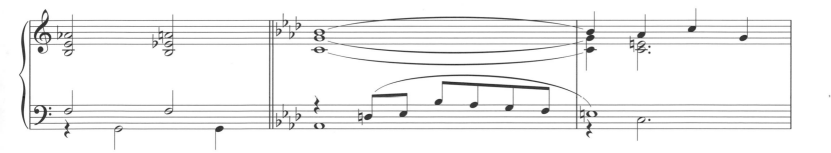

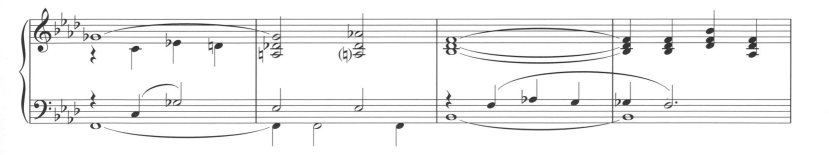

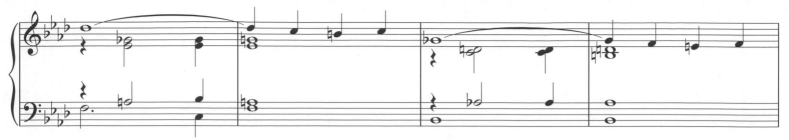

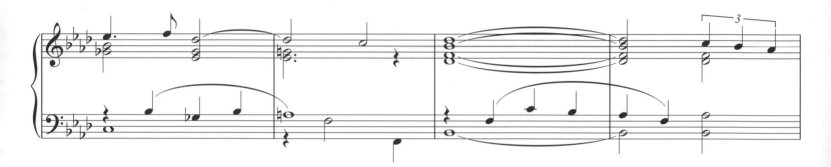

rit.

ALL SYSTEMS GO
from APOLLO 13

Composed by
JAMES HORNER

Moderately

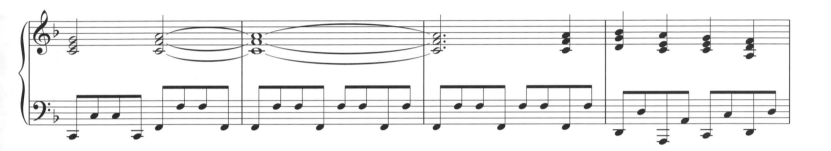

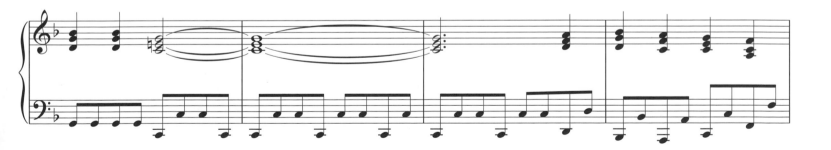

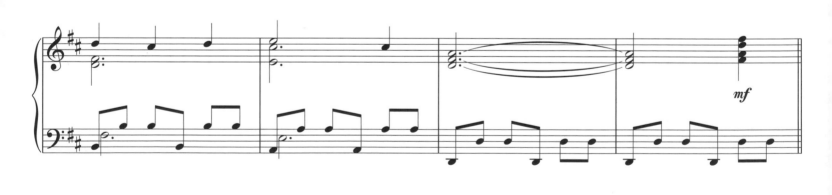

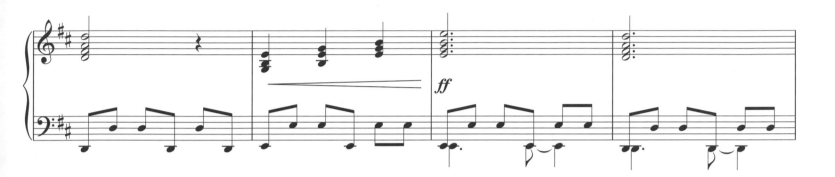

AMERICAN BEAUTY
from AMERICAN BEAUTY

Music by THOMAS NEWMAN

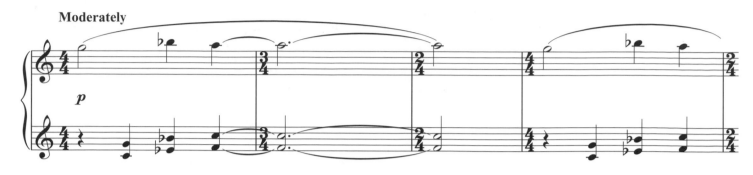

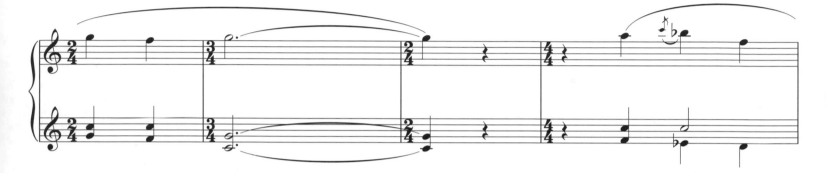

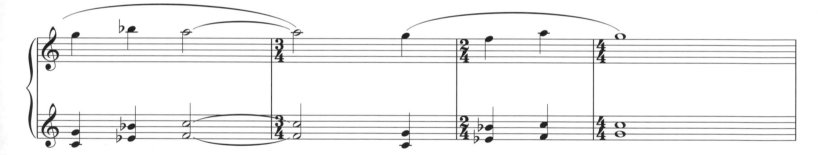

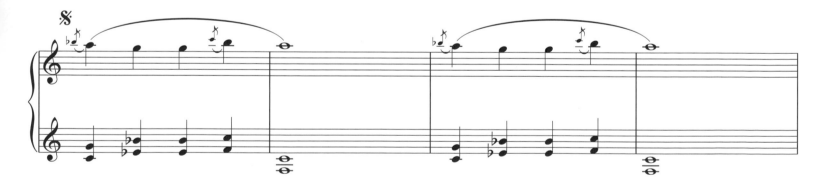

To Coda ⊕

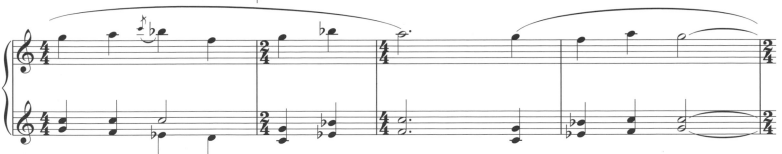

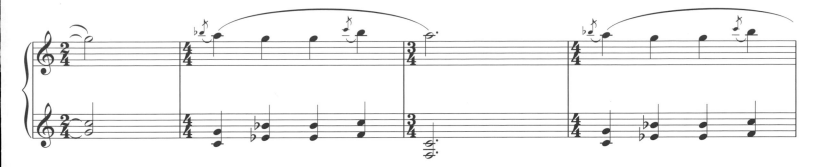

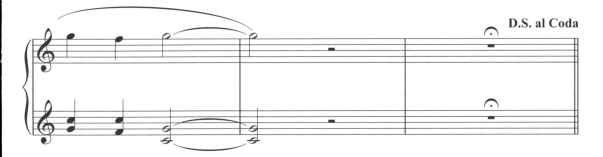

D.S. al Coda

CODA ⊕

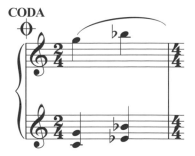

AN AMERICAN SYMPHONY
from MR. HOLLAND'S OPUS

Composed by MICHAEL KAMEN

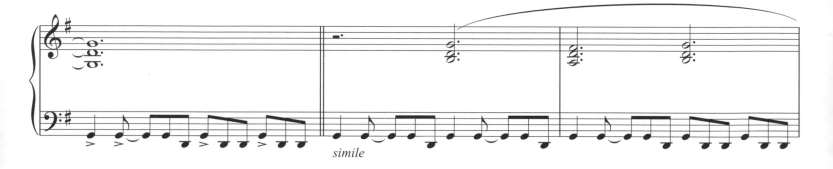

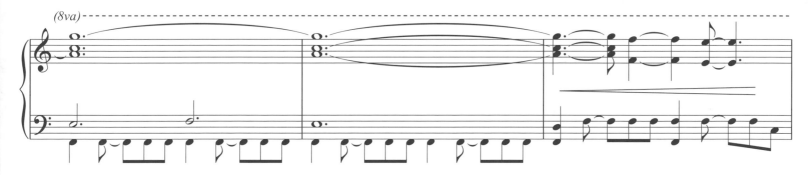

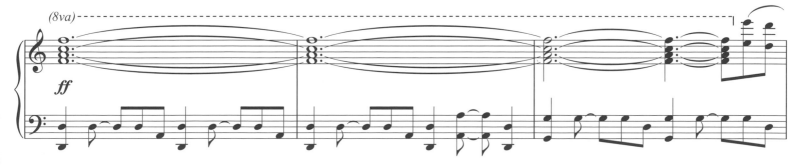

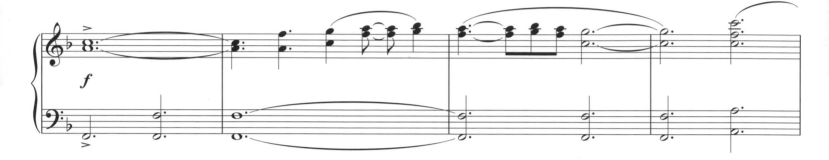

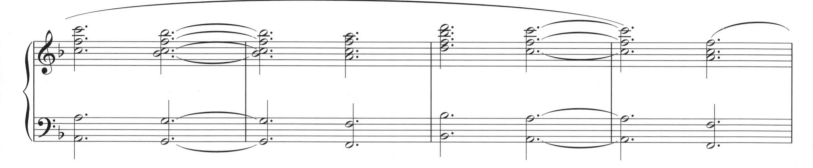

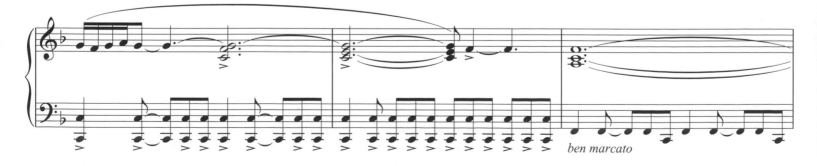

ben marcato

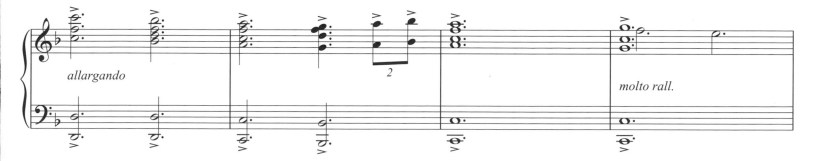

allargando

molto rall.

a tempo

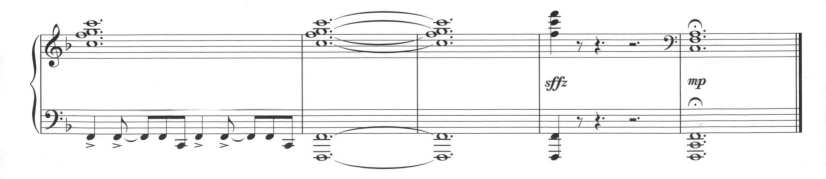

BIG MY SECRET
from THE PIANO

By MICHAEL NYMAN

Molto adagio con rubato (♪ = 50-64)

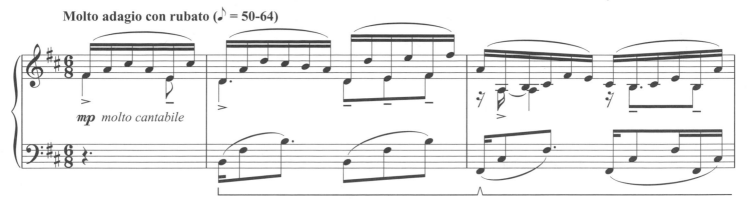

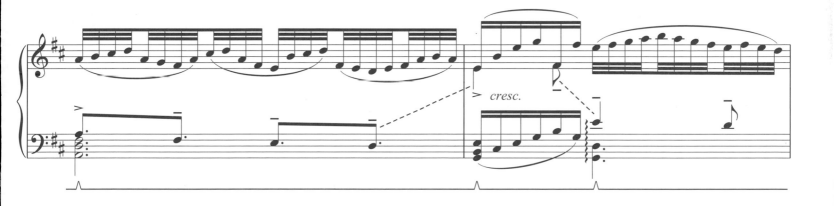

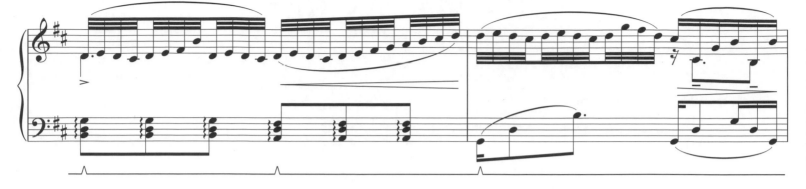

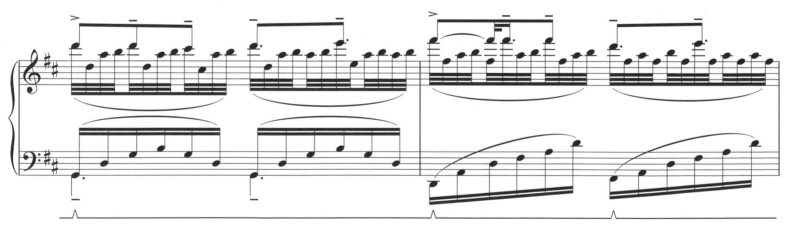

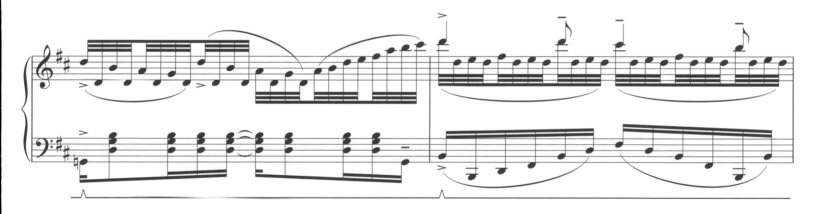

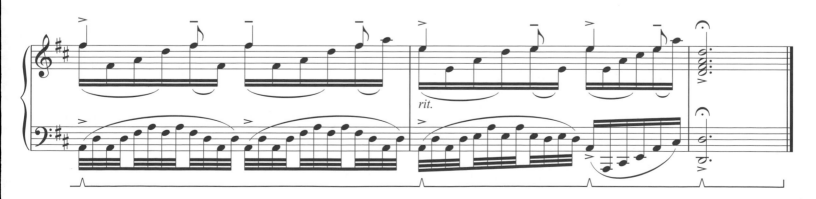

BELLA'S LULLABY

from the Summit Entertainment film TWILIGHT

Composed by
CARTER BURWELL

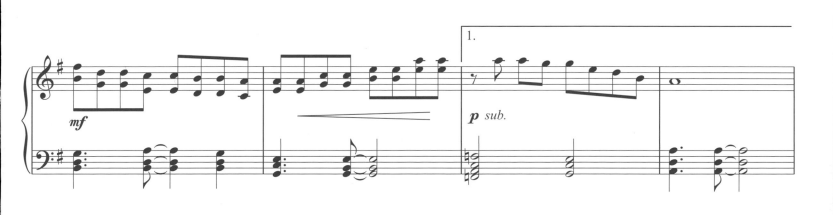

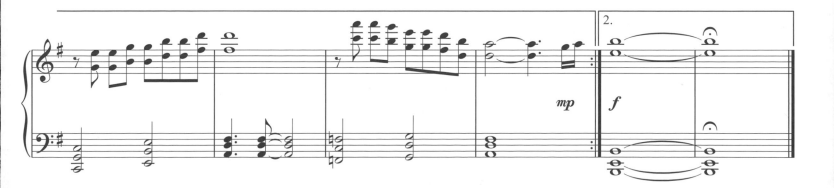

BREAKFAST AT TIFFANY'S
Theme from the Paramount Picture BREAKFAST AT TIFFANY'S

Music by HENRY MANCINI

Moderately, with expression

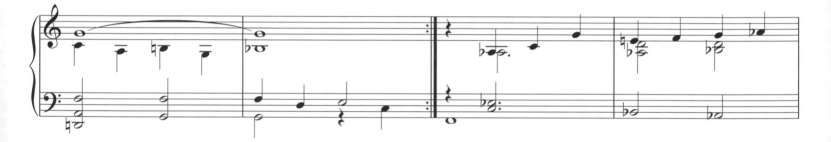

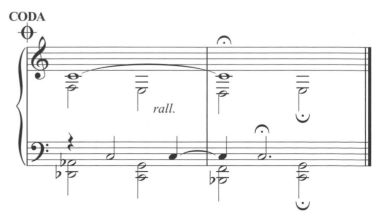

BRIAN'S SONG
Theme from the Screen Gems Television Production BRIAN'S SONG

Music by MICHEL LEGRAND

Moderately, expressively

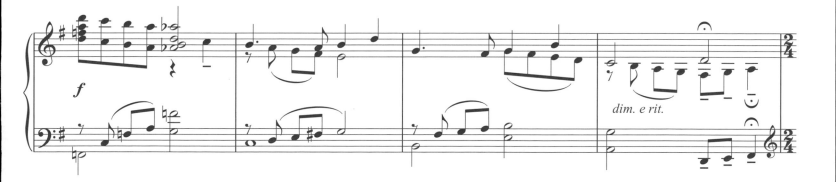

THE CHAIRMAN'S WALTZ
from MEMOIRS OF A GEISHA

By JOHN WILLIAMS

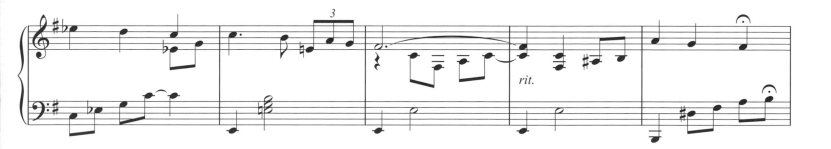

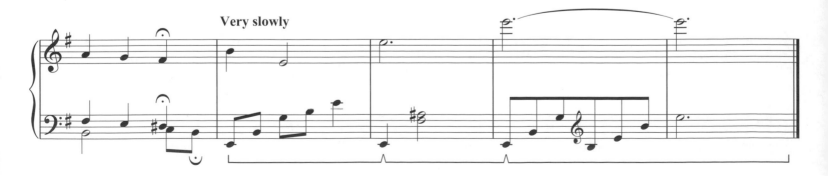

THE CIDER HOUSE RULES

(Main Titles)

from the Miramax Motion Picture THE CIDER HOUSE RULES

By RACHEL PORTMAN

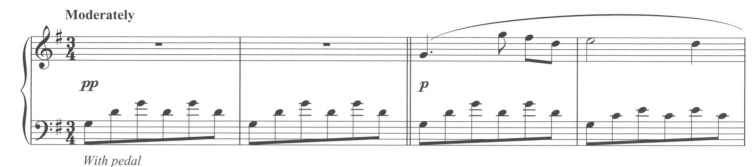

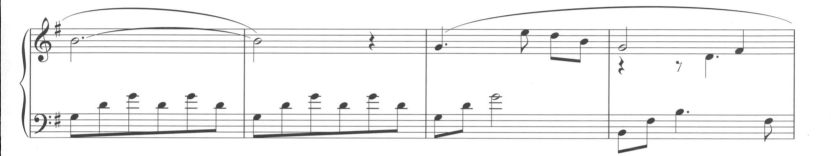

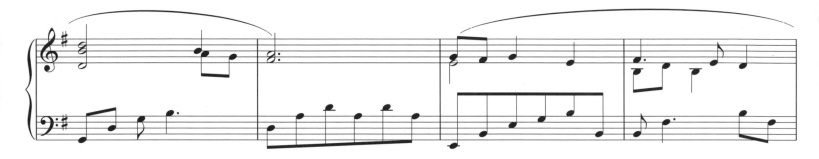

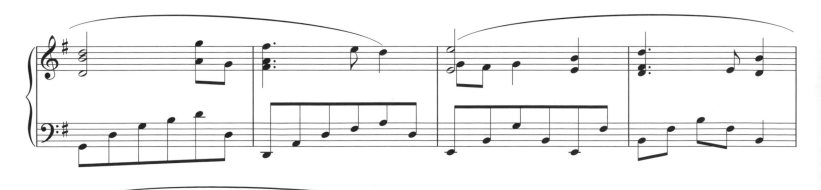

cresc.

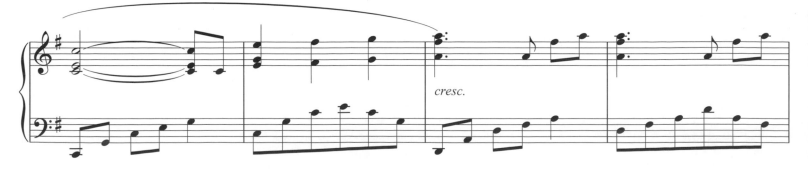

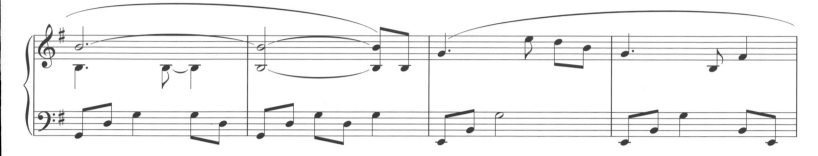

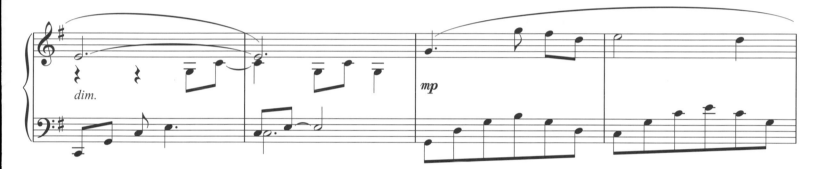

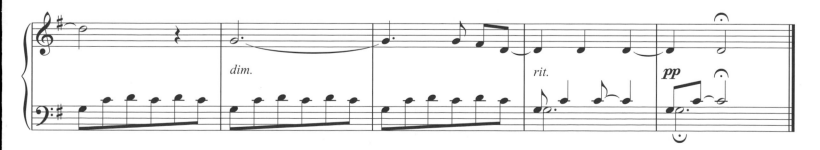

CHOCOLAT
(Main Titles)
from the Motion Picture CHOCOLAT

By RACHEL PORTMAN

Slowly, expressively

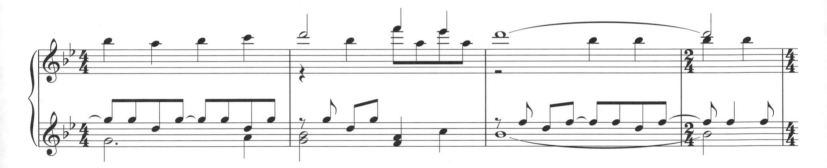

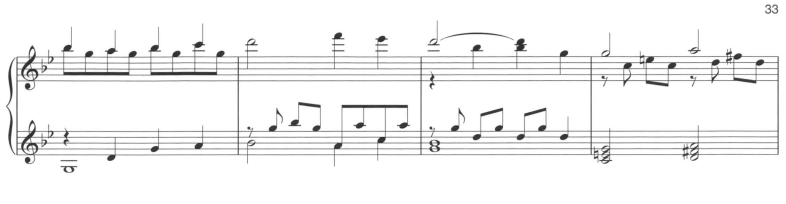

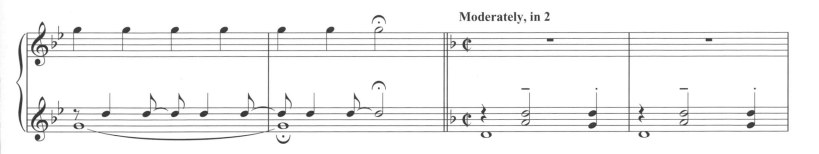

Moderately, in 2

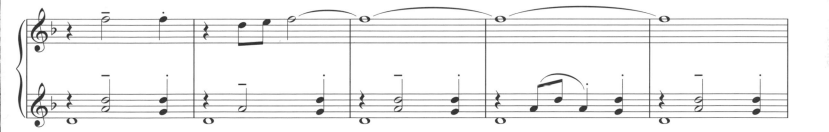

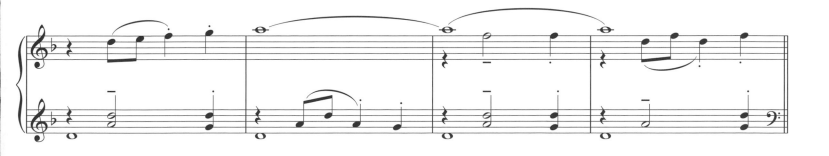

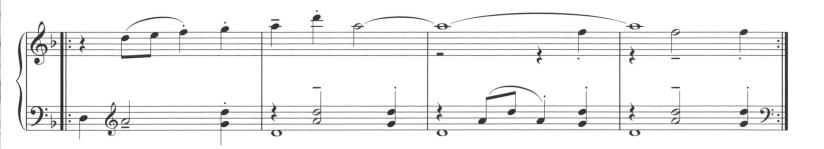

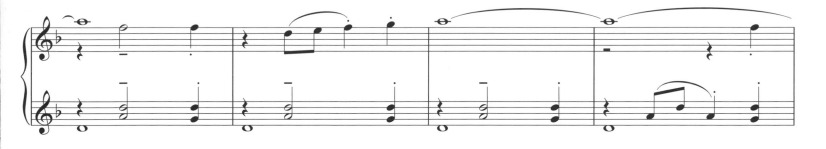

rit.

CINEMA PARADISO

from CINEMA PARADISO

By ENNIO MORRICONE
and ANDREA MORRICONE

Simply, with feeling

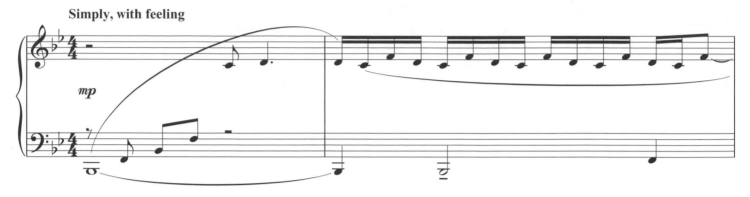

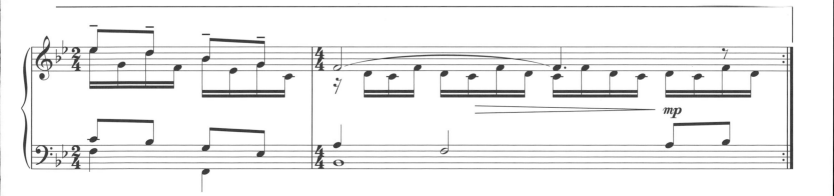

THE CLOCKS
from the Paramount Motion Picture HUGO

By HOWARD SHORE
Contains an excerpt from "Aubade Charmeuse"
by JEAN PEYRONNIN

Moderately ($\quad$ = 108)

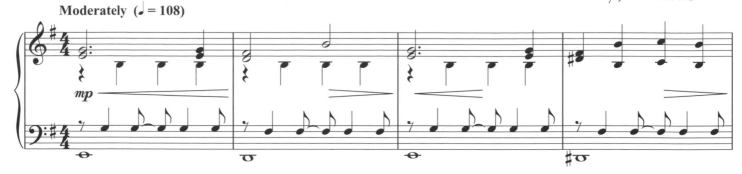

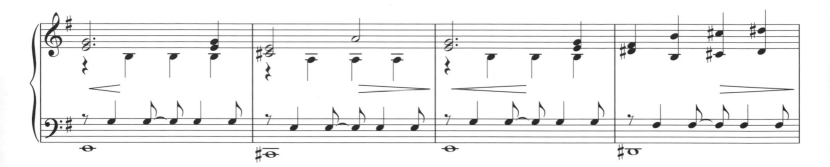

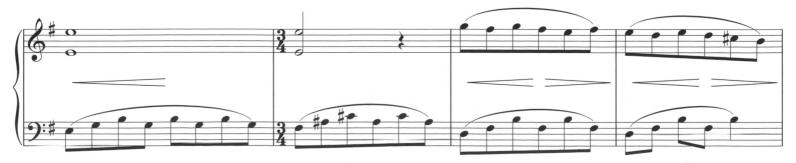

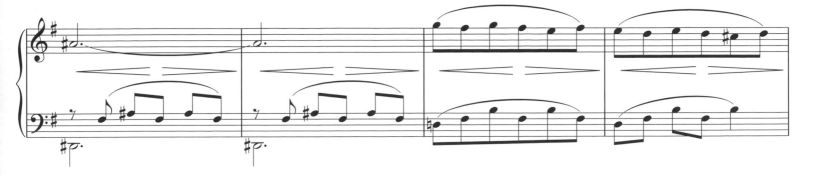

Slightly faster (♩ = 120)

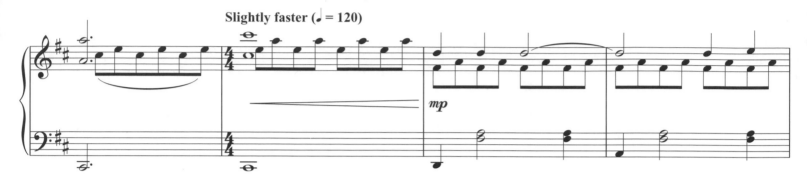

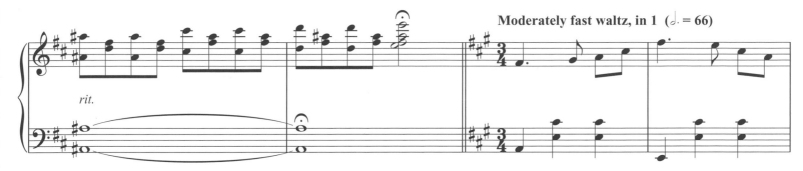

Moderately fast waltz, in 1 ($\bullet . = 66$)

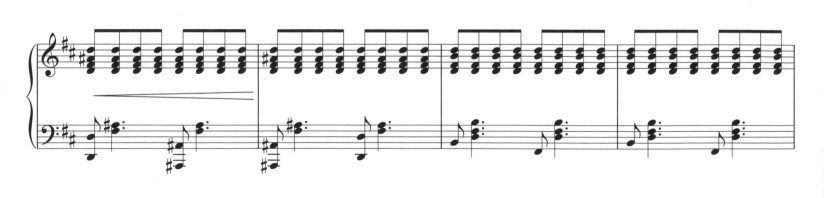

COUSINS
(Love Theme)
from the Paramount Picture COUSINS

Music by ANGELO BADALAMENTI

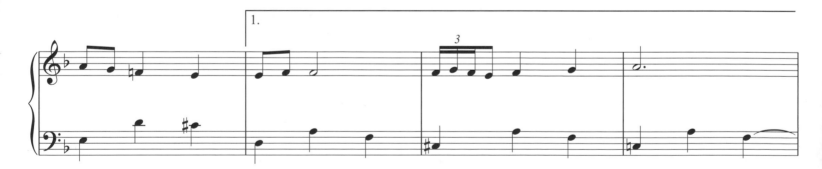

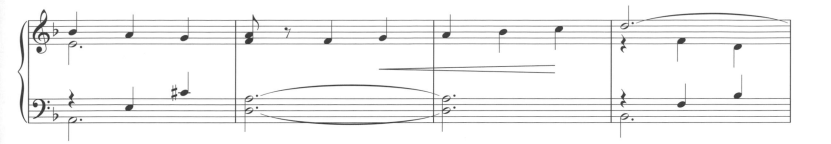

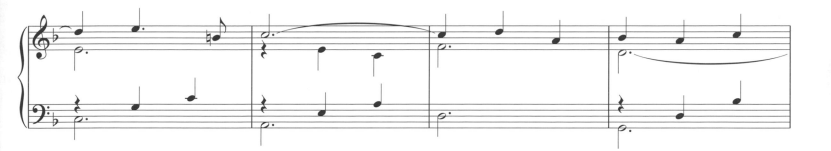

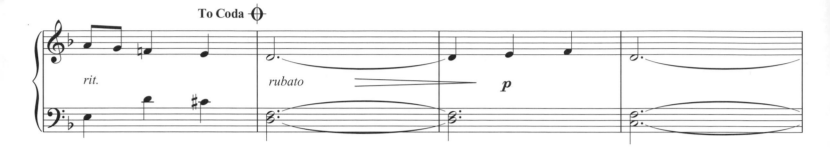

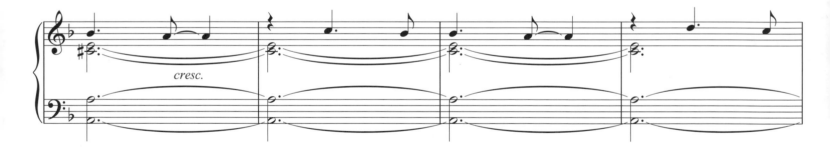

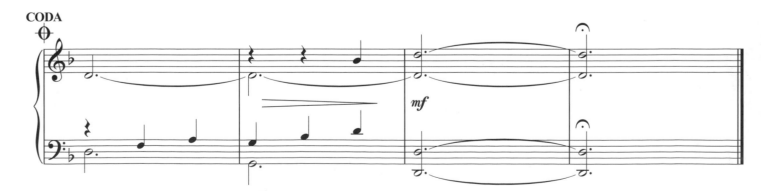

FALLING SLOWLY
from the Motion Picture ONCE

Words and Music by GLEN HANSARD
and MARKETA IRGLOVA

Slowly (♩ = 69)

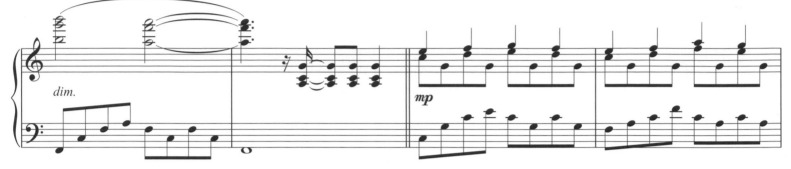

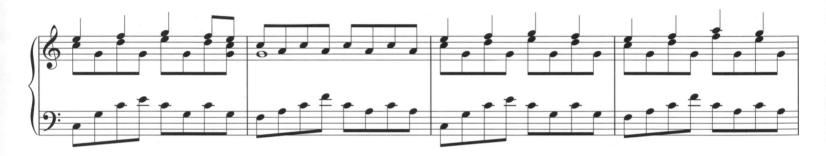

DAWN
from PRIDE AND PREJUDICE

By DARIO MARIANELLI

Freely　　　　　　　　　　　　　**Moderately slow, very expressively**

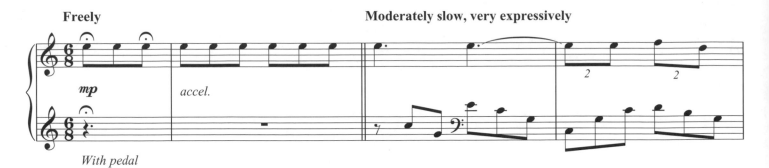

Moderately fast, with motion

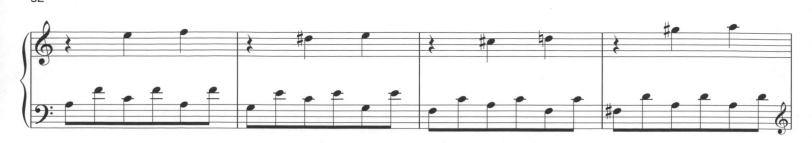

Slightly slower

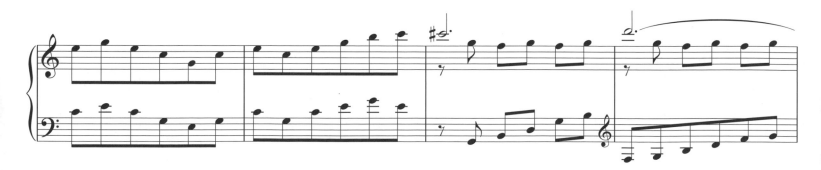

Slowly

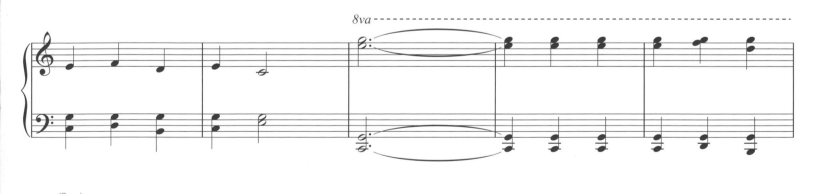

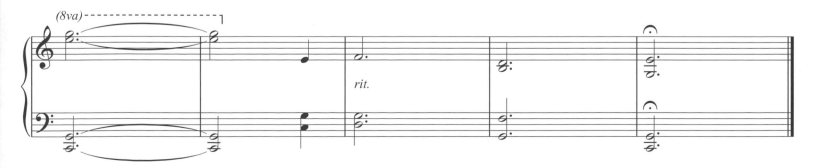

DREAMS TO DREAM
(Finale Version)
from the Universal Motion Picture AN AMERICAN TAIL: FIEVEL GOES WEST

Words and Music by JAMES HORNER
and WILL JENNINGS

To Coda

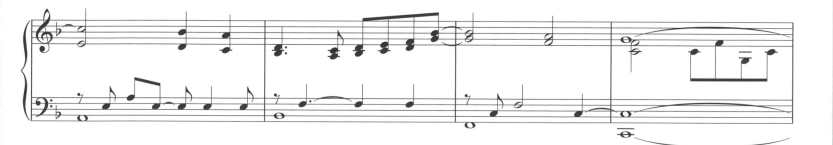

EARTH
from the DreamWorks film GLADIATOR

Written by HANS ZIMMER

Moderately

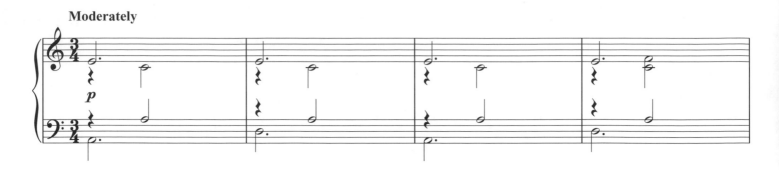

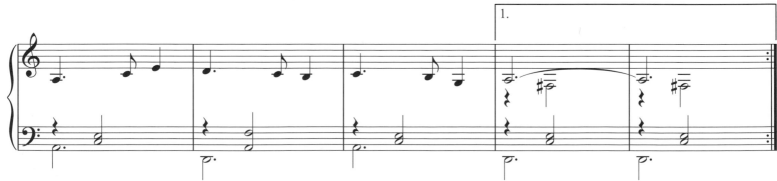

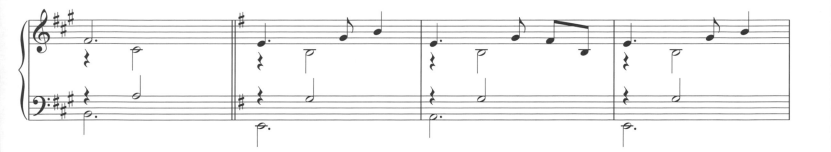

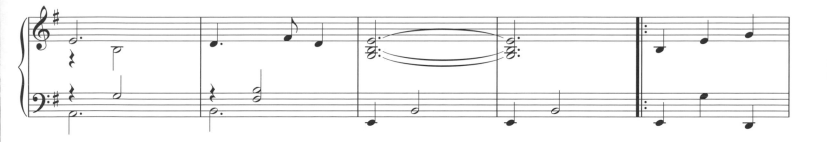

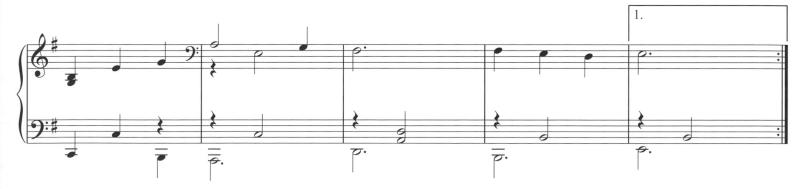

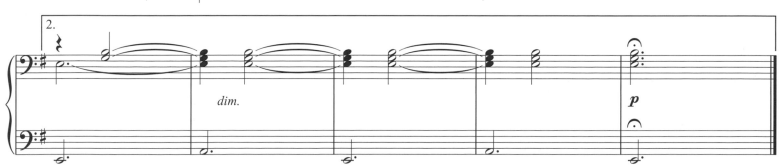

THE ENGLISH PATIENT
from THE ENGLISH PATIENT

Written by GABRIEL YARED

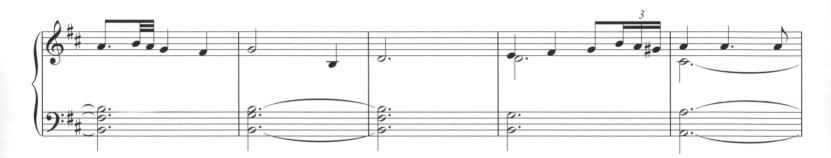

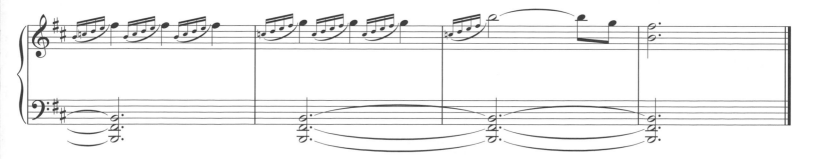

FAR AND AWAY

(Main Theme)

from the Universal Motion Picture FAR AND AWAY

Composed by JOHN WILLIAMS

Moderately

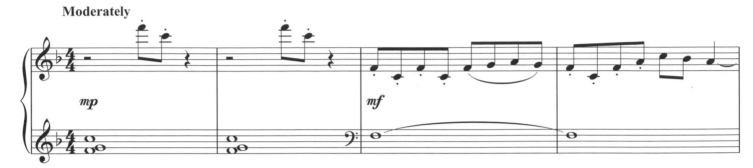

Sweetly, slightly slower

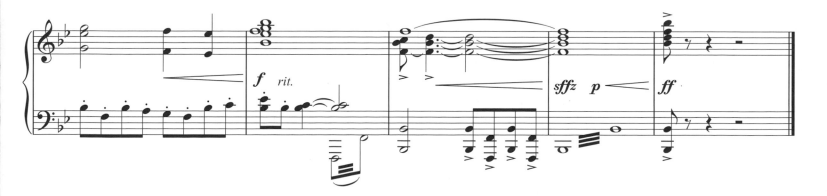

THEME FROM "FATAL ATTRACTION"

from the Paramount Motion Picture FATAL ATTRACTION

Music by MAURICE JARRE

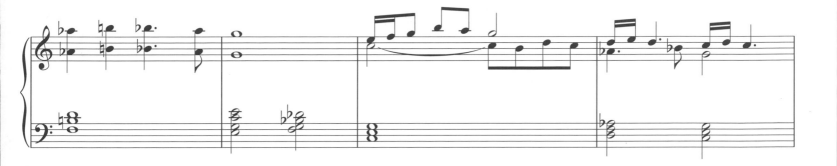

THE FIRM – MAIN TITLE

from the Paramount Motion Picture THE FIRM

By DAVE GRUSIN

Moderately, with a steady pulse

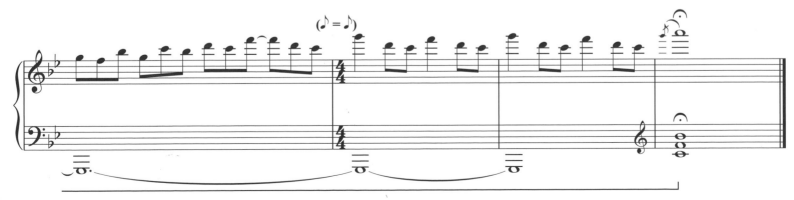

LOVE THEME FROM "FLASHDANCE"

from the Paramount Picture FLASHDANCE

Music by GIORGIO MORODER

rit.

FORREST GUMP – MAIN TITLE
(Feather Theme)
from the Paramount Motion Picture FORREST GUMP

Music by ALAN SILVESTRI

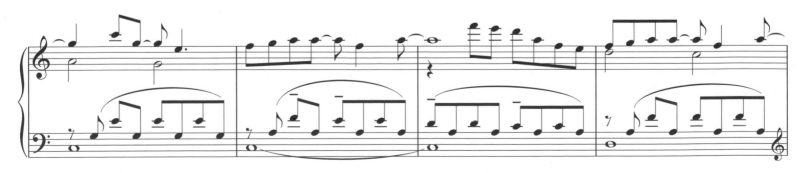

(lightly)

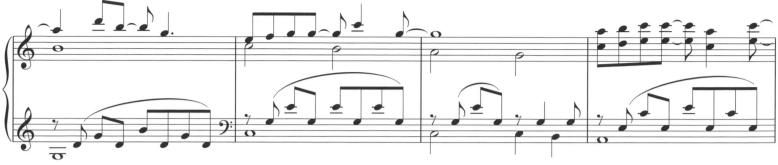

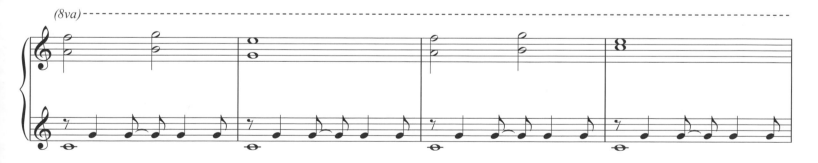

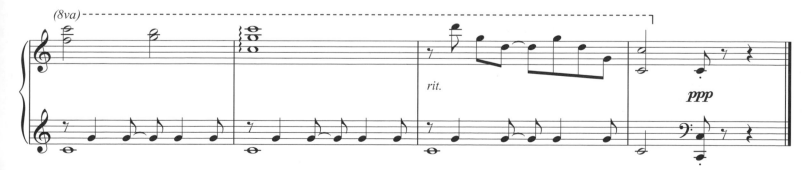

GABRIEL'S OBOE
from the Motion Picture THE MISSION

Music by ENNIO MORRICONE

Slowly, expressively

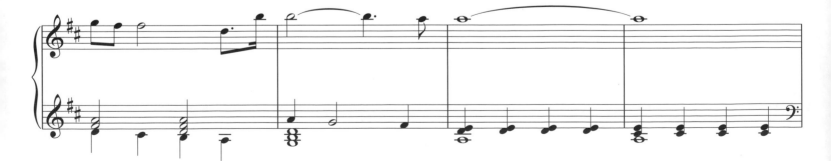

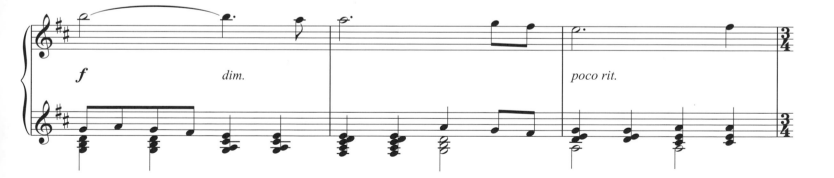

GALE'S THEME
(Main Title)
from THE RIVER WILD

By JERRY GOLDSMITH

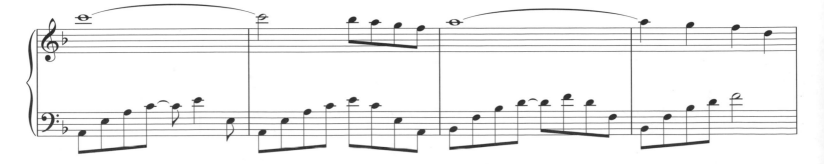

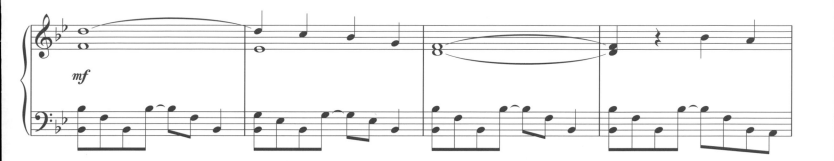

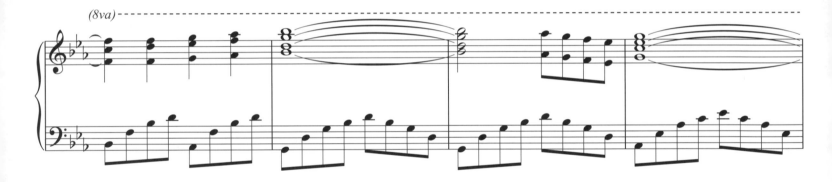

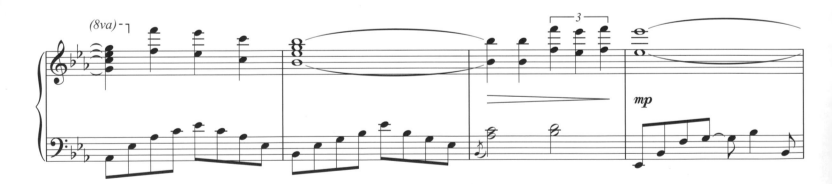

GEORGE VALENTIN
from the Motion Picture THE ARTIST

Composed by LUDOVIC BOURCE

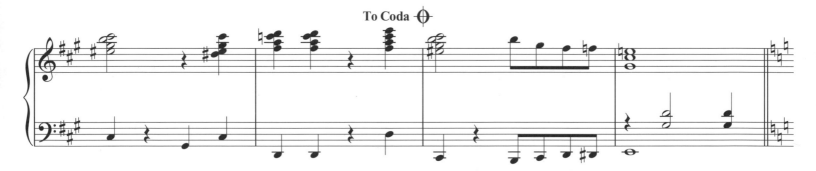

To Coda

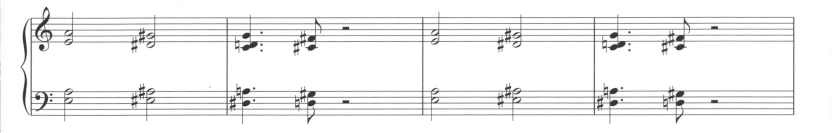

Play 4 times

D.S. al Coda

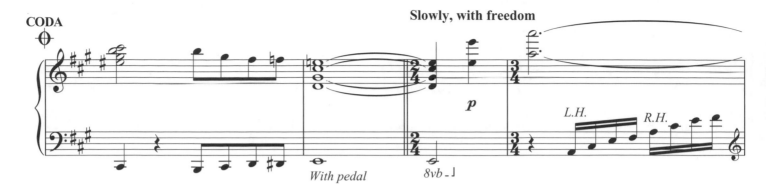

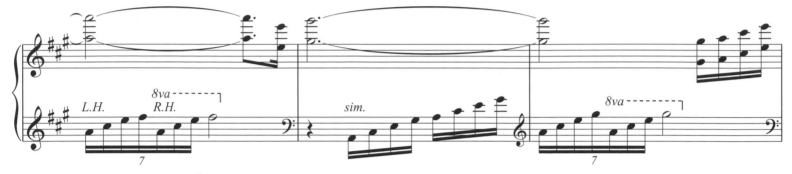

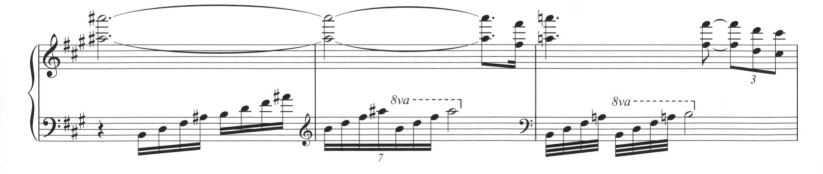

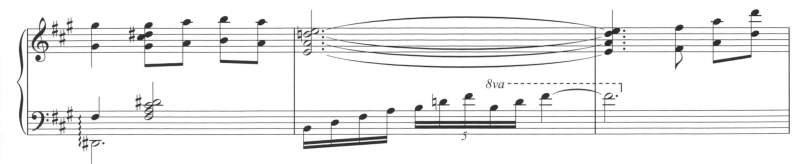

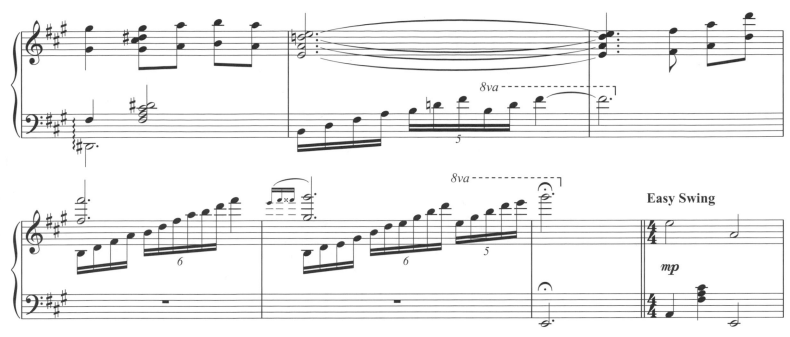

GEORGIANA
from PRIDE AND PREJUDICE

By DARIO MARIANELLI

Moderately fast, in 4

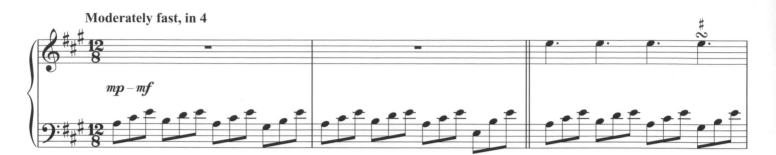

R.H. over L.H.

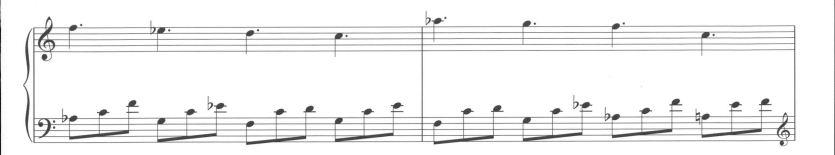

rit.

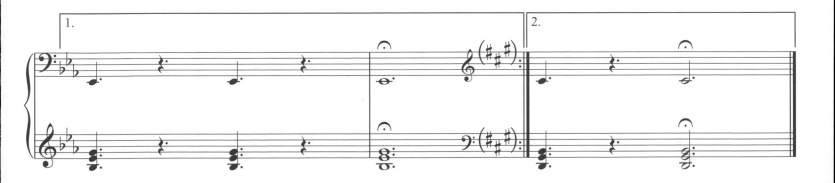

THE GODFATHER

(Love Theme)
from the Paramount Picture THE GODFATHER

By NINO ROTA

Slowly and expressively

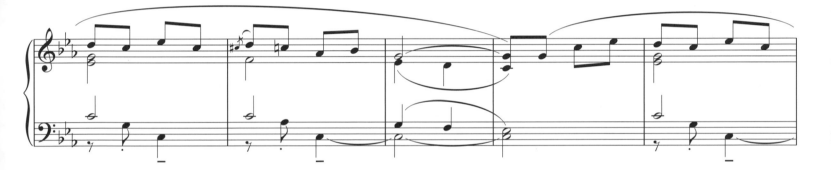
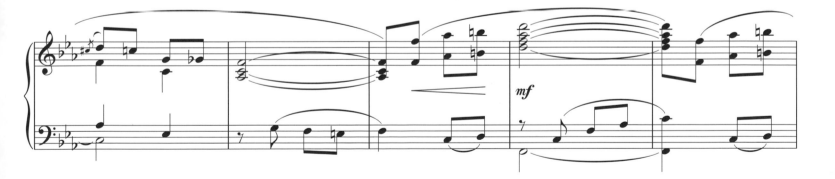

THE GUNS OF NAVARONE

from THE GUNS OF NAVARONE

Words and Music by DIMITRI TIOMKIN
and PAUL WEBSTER

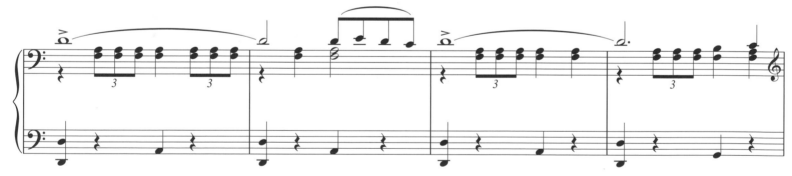

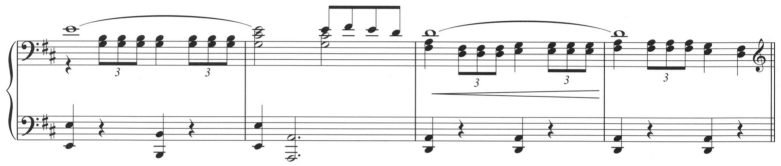

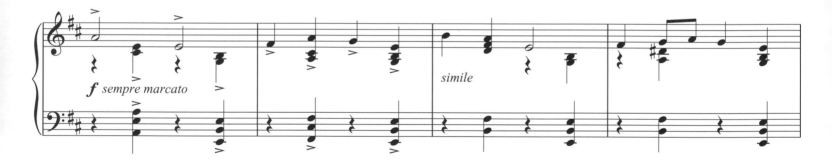

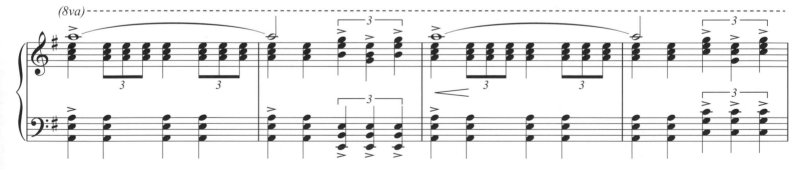

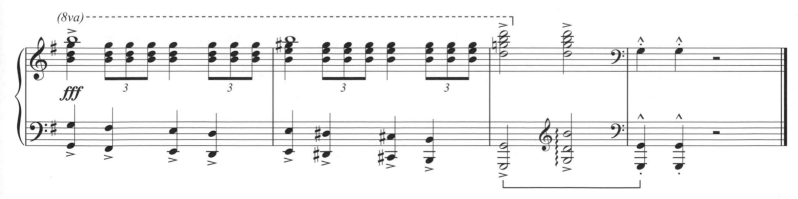

THE HEART ASKS PLEASURE FIRST

from THE PIANO

By MICHAEL NYMAN

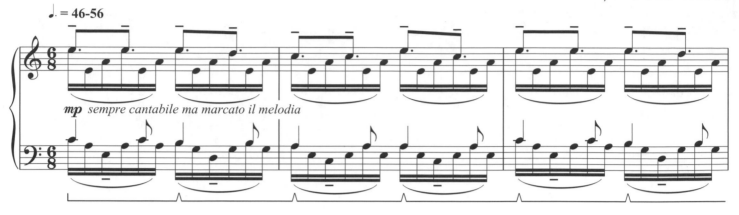

mp sempre cantabile ma marcato il melodia

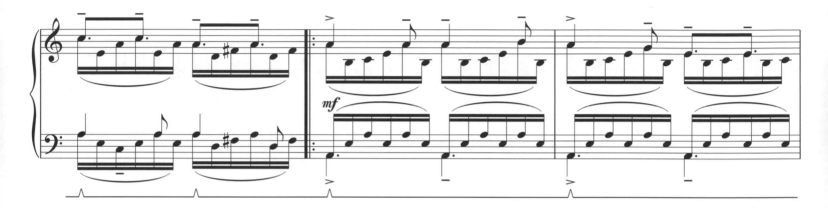

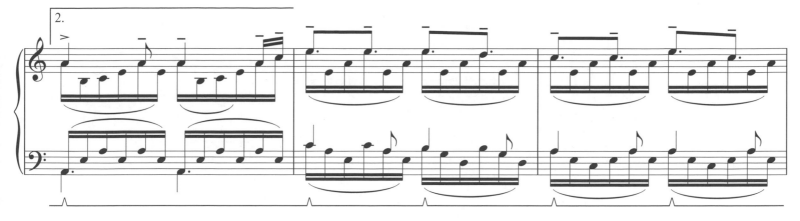

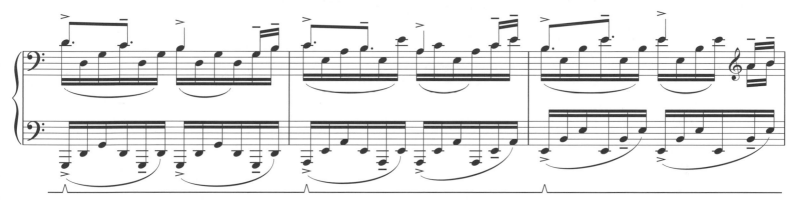

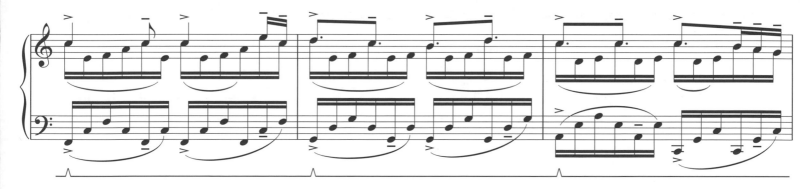

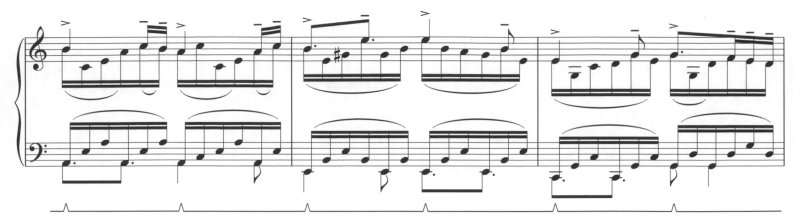

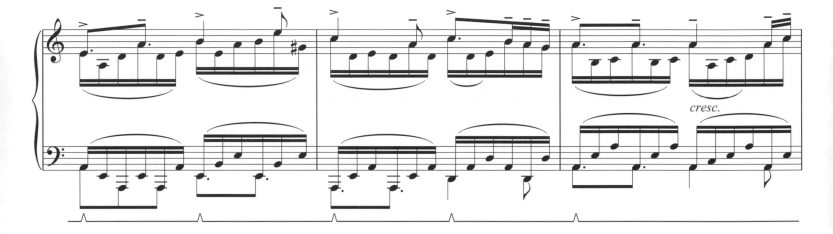

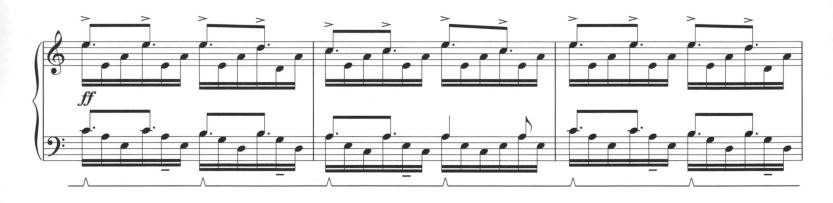

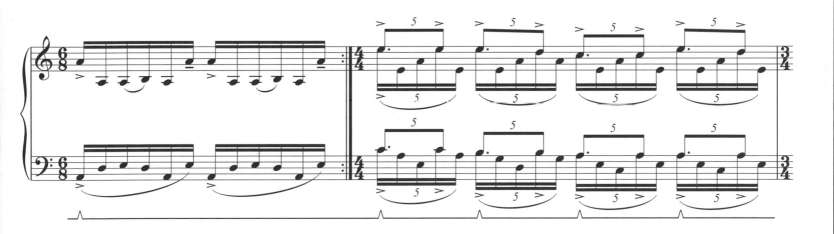

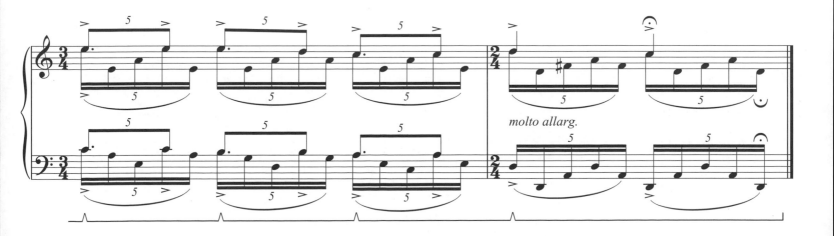

HEAVEN CAN WAIT
(Love Theme)
from the Paramount Motion Picture HEAVEN CAN WAIT

Music by DAVE GRUSIN

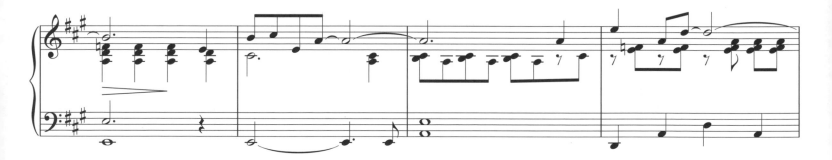

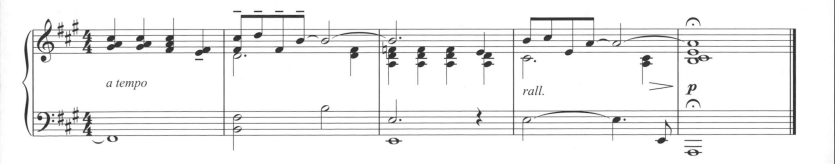

HYMN TO THE FALLEN

from the Paramount and DreamWorks Motion Picture SAVING PRIVATE RYAN

Music by JOHN WILLIAMS

Slowly, reverently

Slightly faster

Broadly and expansively

IL POSTINO
(The Postman)
from IL POSTINO

Music by LUIS BACALOV

Moderately

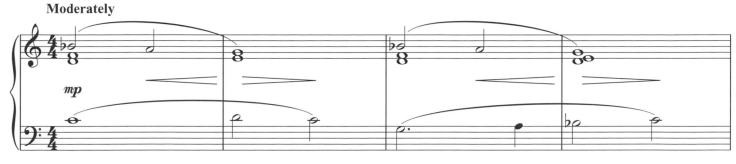

With pedal

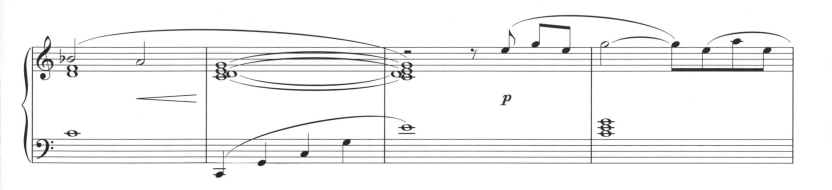

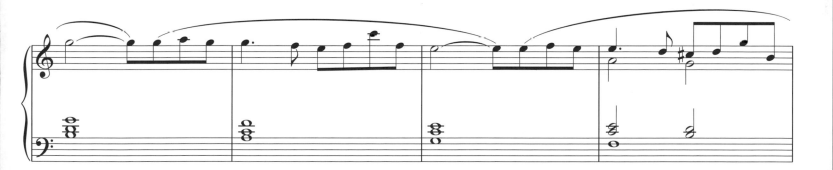

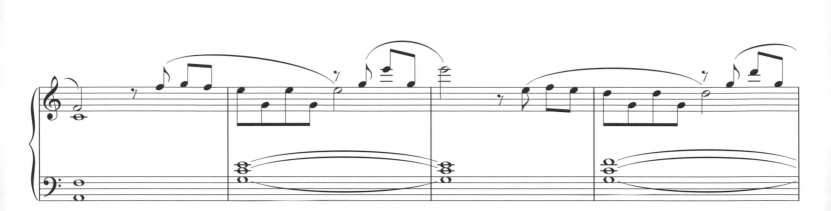

Tempo I

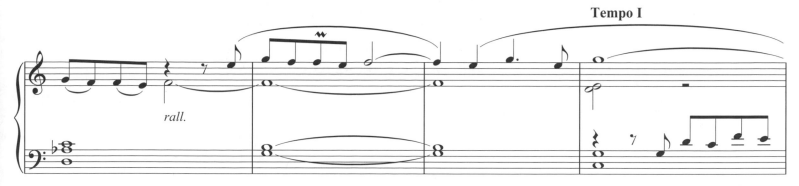

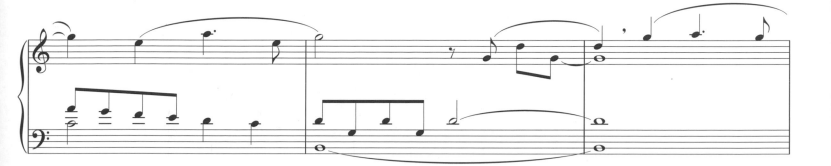

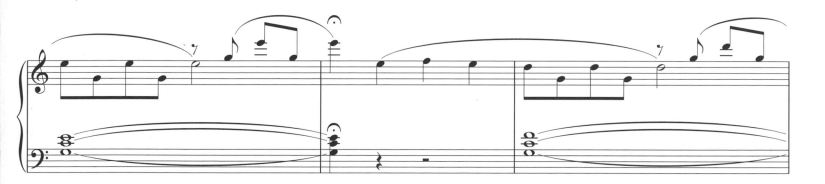

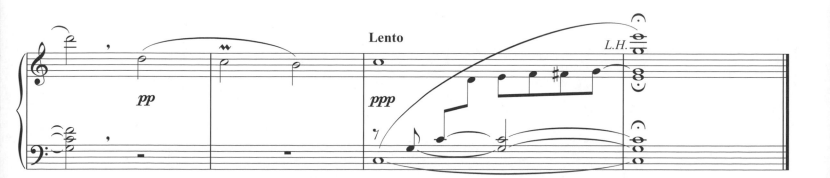

INDECENT PROPOSAL

(Main Title)

from INDECENT PROPOSAL

By JOHN BARRY

Slowly

mp

With pedal

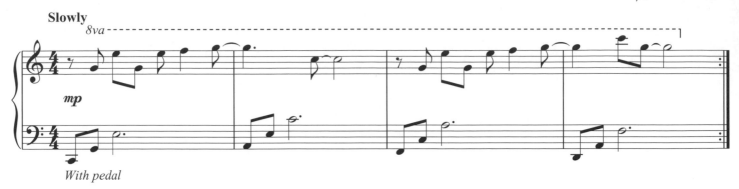

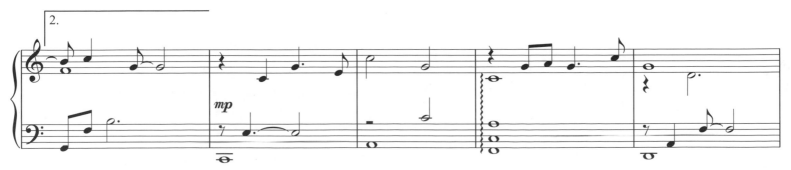

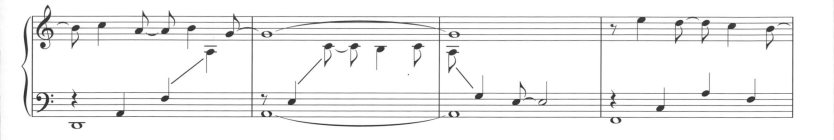

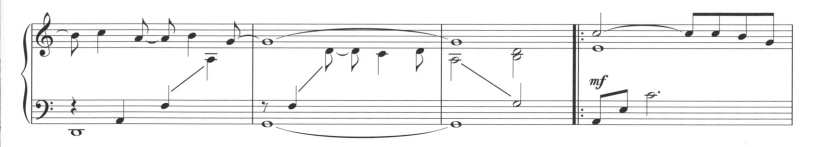

IT MIGHT BE YOU
Theme from TOOTSIE

Words by ALAN and MARILYN BERGMAN
Music by DAVE GRUSIN

Moderately slow

JESSICA'S THEME
(Breaking in the Colt)
from THE MAN FROM SNOWY RIVER

By BRUCE ROWLAND

To Coda

D.S. al Coda

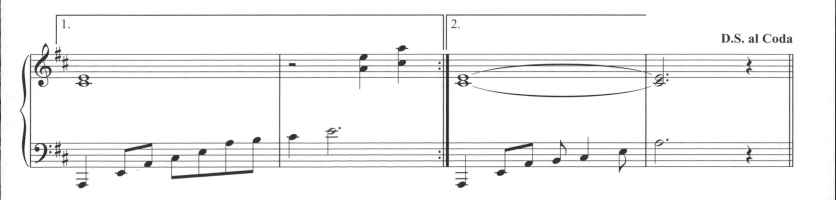

CODA

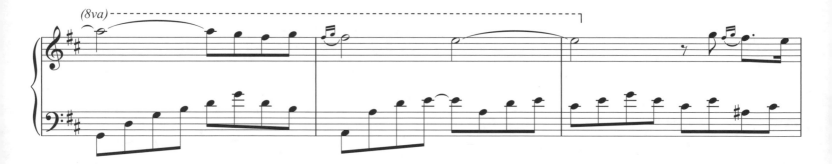

JACOB'S THEME
from the Summit Entertainment film THE TWILIGHT SAGA: ECLIPSE

Composed by HOWARD SHORE

Rubato

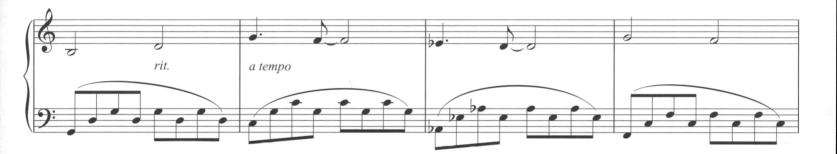

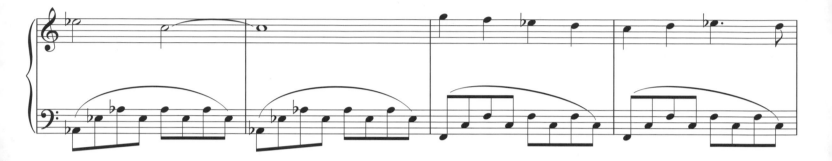

THE JOHN DUNBAR THEME

from DANCES WITH WOLVES

By JOHN BARRY

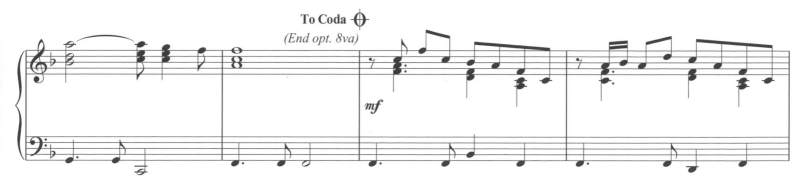

CODA

THEME FROM "JURASSIC PARK"

from the Universal Motion Picture JURASSIC PARK

Composed by JOHN WILLIAMS

KYRIE FOR THE MAGDALENE

from THE DA VINCI CODE

By RICHARD HARVEY

Moderately

With pedal

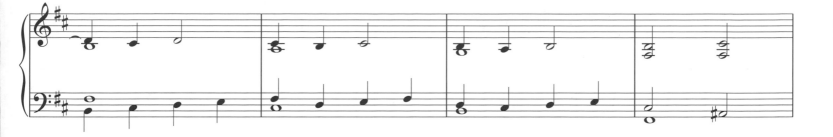

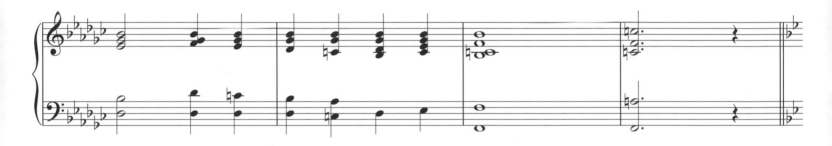

LA PASSERELLA DI ADDIO

Theme from the film 8½

Music by NINO ROTA

Allegro moderato

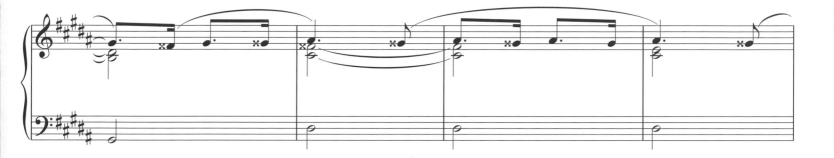

rall.

LA VALSE D'AMELIE
from AMELIE

By YANN TIERSEN

Slowly (♩ = 48)

Flowing (♩. = 60)

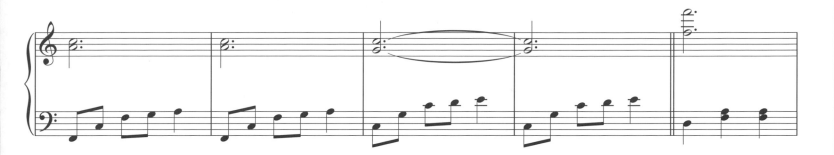

LAST OF THE MOHICANS
(Main Theme)
from the Twentieth Century Fox Motion Picture THE LAST OF THE MOHICANS

By TREVOR JONES

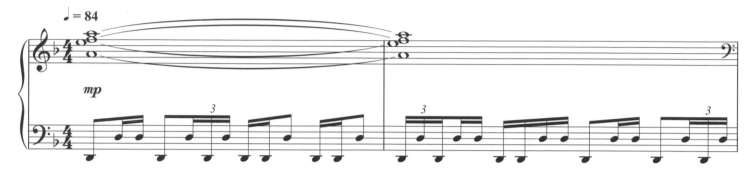

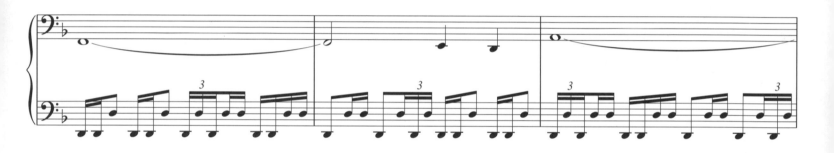

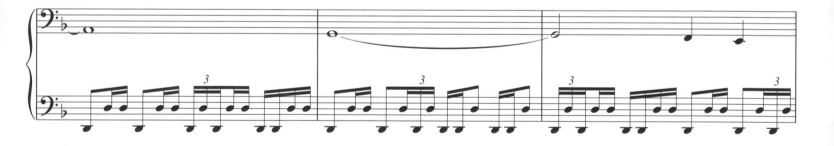

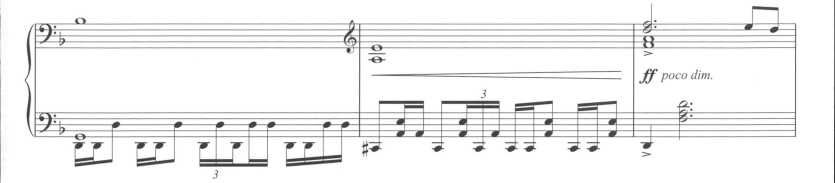

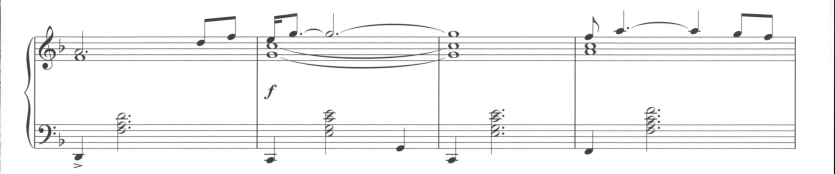

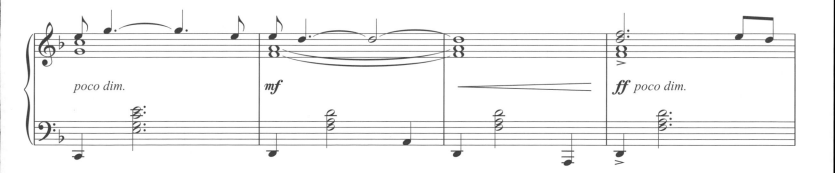

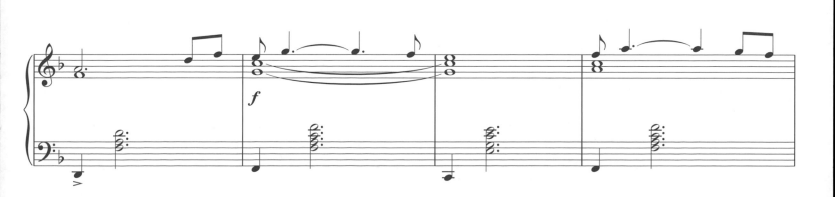

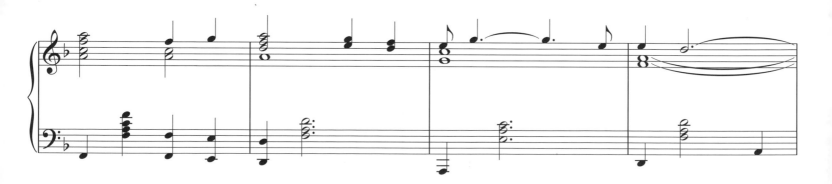

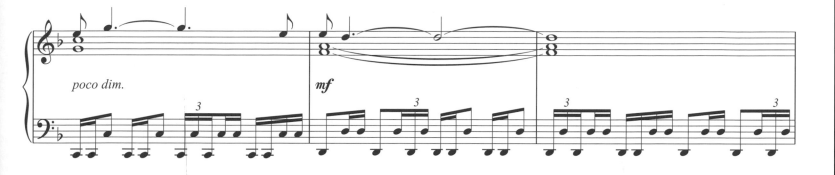

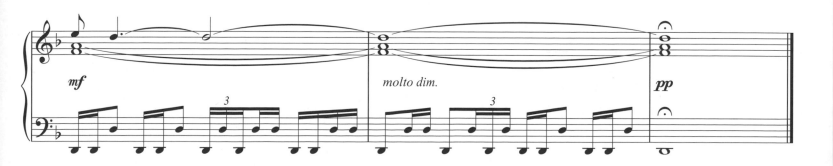

THEME FROM
"LAWRENCE OF ARABIA"

from LAWRENCE OF ARABIA

By MAURICE JARRE

With fire

Slowly, with expression

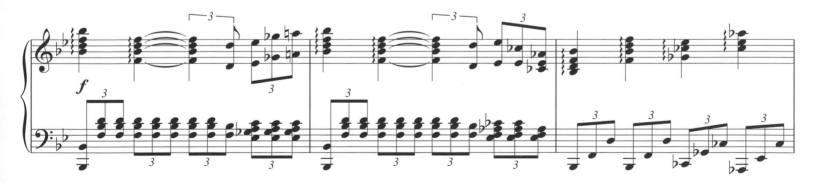

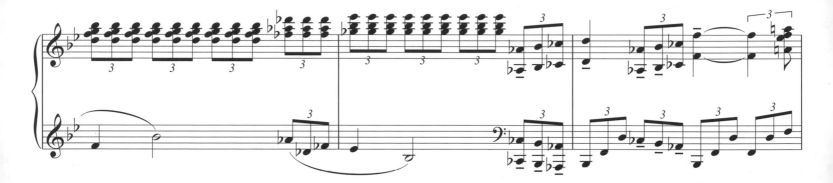

With fire

LOVE STORY
Theme from the Paramount Picture LOVE STORY

Music by FRANCIS LAI

A LOVE BEFORE TIME

from the Motion Picture CROUCHING TIGER, HIDDEN DRAGON

Words and Music by KEVIN YI,
TAN DUN and JORGE CALANDRELLI

Freely, expressively

With pedal

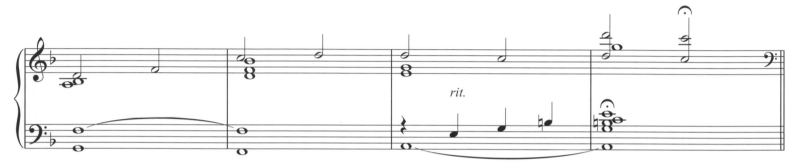

Relaxed half-time feel

To Coda ⊕

D.S. al Coda

CODA

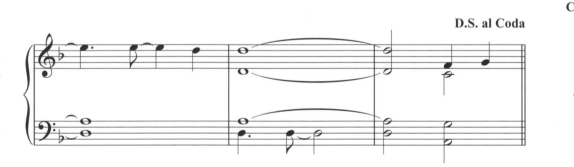

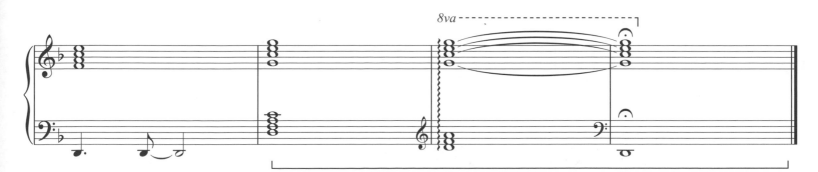

THE LUDLOWS
from TriStar Pictures' LEGENDS OF THE FALL

Composed by JAMES HORNER

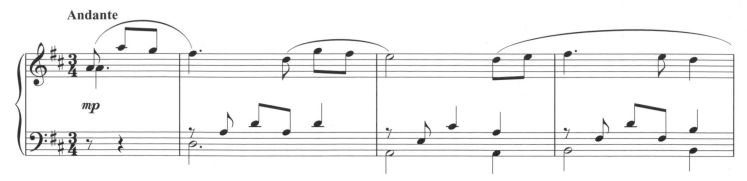

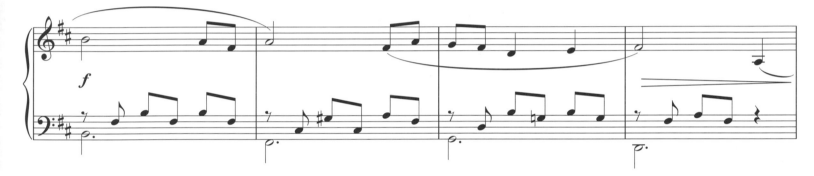

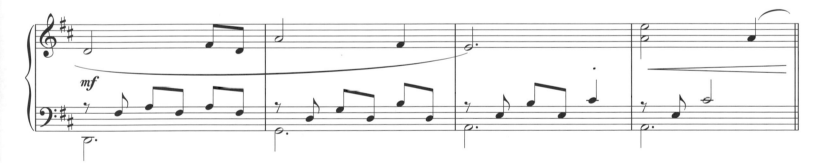

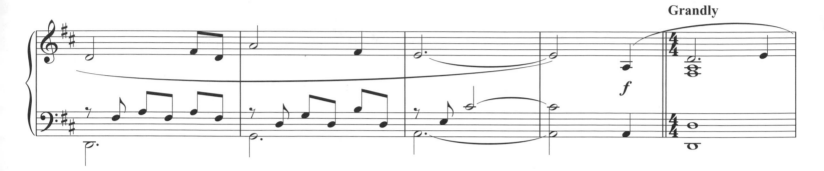

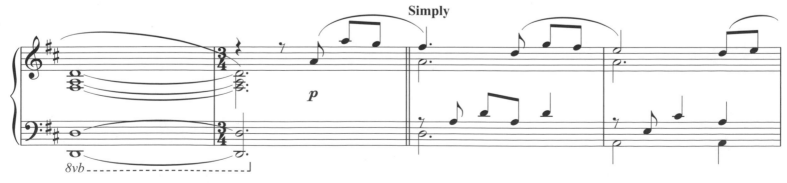

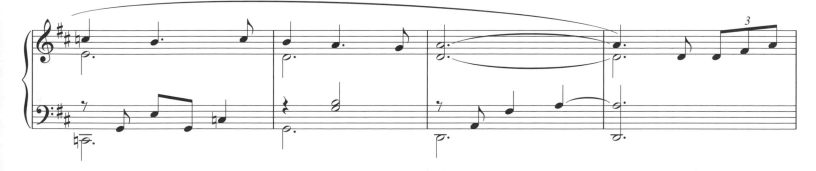

MAESTRO
from THE HOLIDAY

By HANS ZIMMER

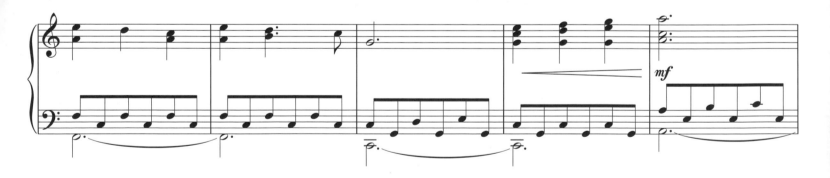

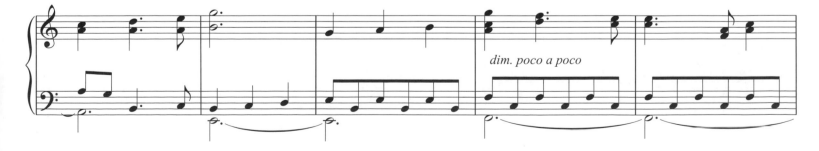

Slowly, in 2

Play 4 times

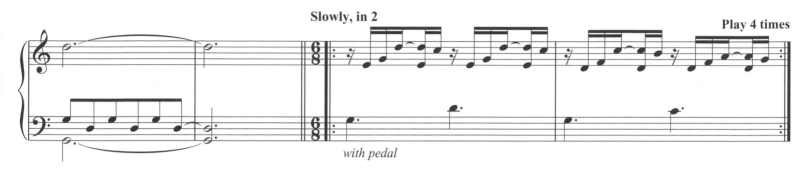

with pedal

Very slowly

THE MAN FROM SNOWY RIVER
(Main Title Theme)
from THE MAN FROM SNOWY RIVER

By BRUCE ROWLAND

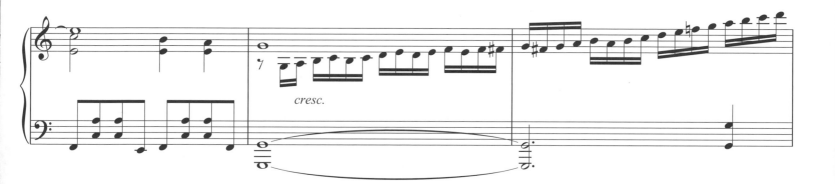

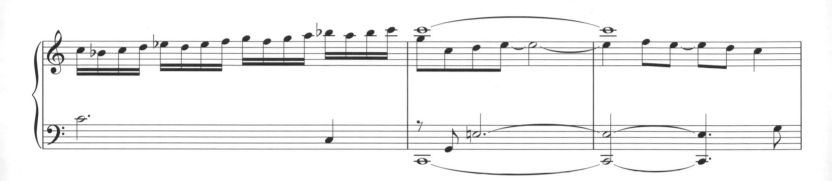

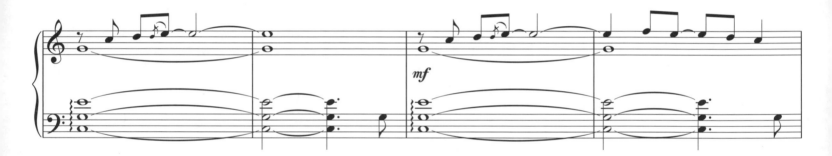

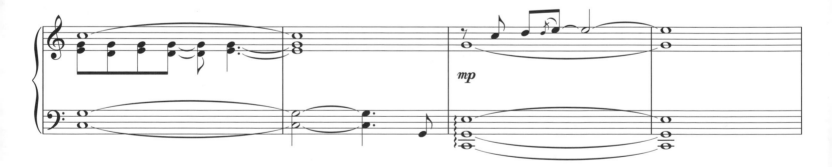

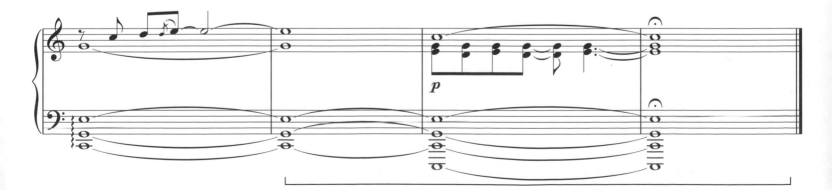

MORE
(Ti guarderò nel cuore)
from the film MONDO CANE

Music by NINO OLIVIERO and RIZ ORTOLANI
Italian Lyrics by MARCELLO CIORCIOLINI
English Lyrics by NORMAN NEWELL

Moderate Bossa Nova

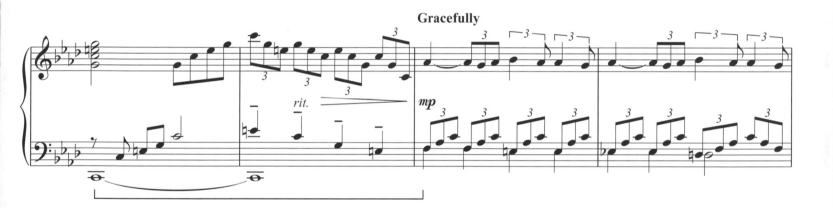

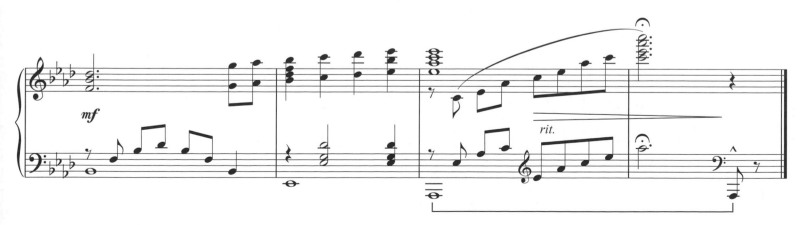

MY FATHER'S FAVORITE
from SENSE AND SENSIBILITY

By PATRICK DOYLE

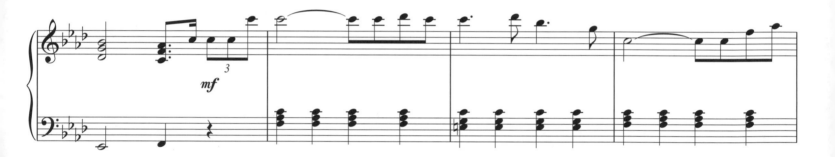

THE NAKED GUN
FROM THE FILES OF POLICE SQUAD!

from the Paramount Picture THE NAKED GUN FROM THE FILES OF POLICE SQUAD

Music by IRA NEWBORN

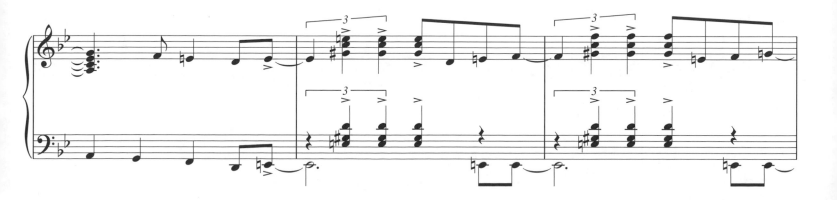

NEVERLAND –
PIANO VARIATIONS IN BLUE
from FINDING NEVERLAND

By A.P. KACZMAREK

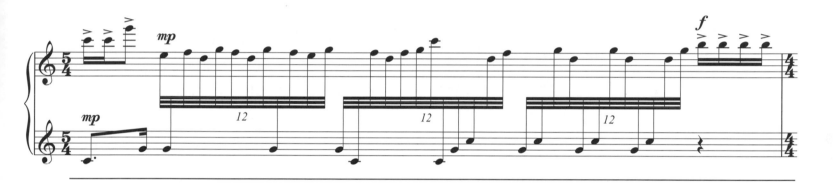

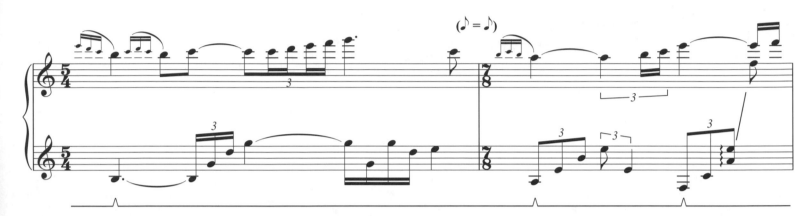

Slowly, freely, in 2

With pedal

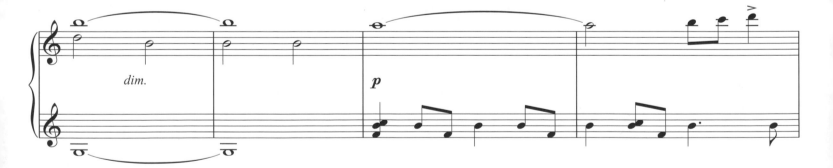

Slowly, in 2 (in time)

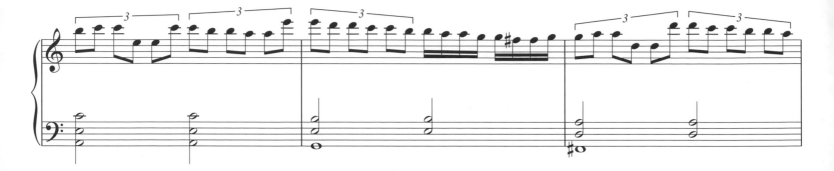

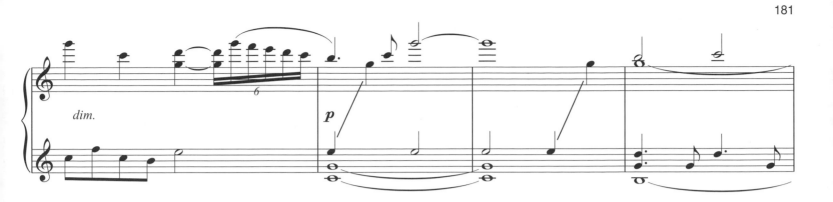

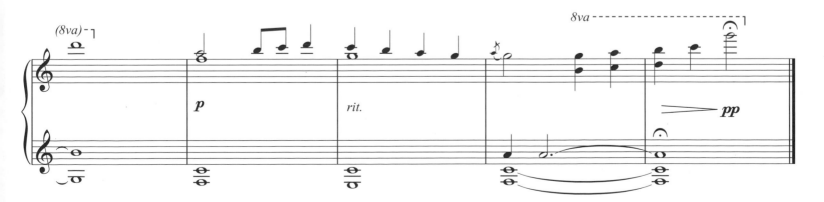

NICHOLAS AND ALEXANDRA
Theme from NICHOLAS AND ALEXANDRA

By RICHARD RODNEY BENNETT

Moderately, flowing

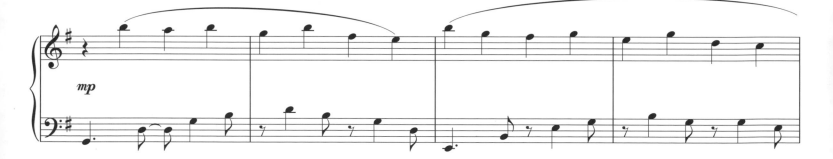

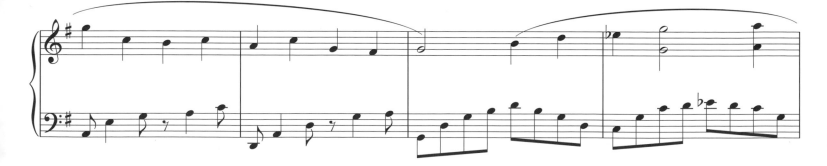

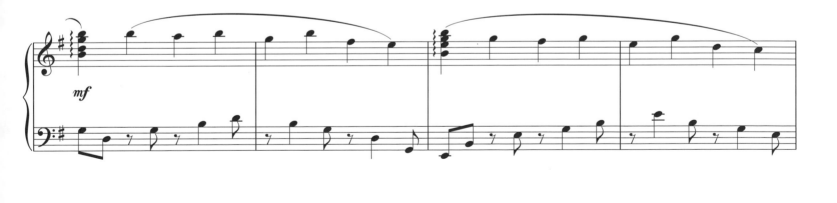

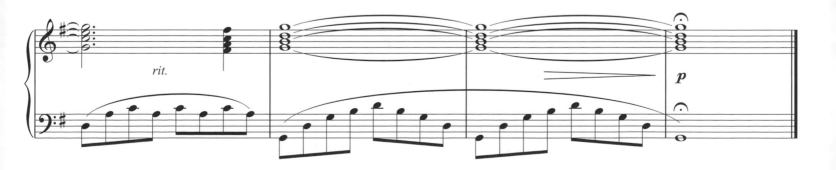

NOW WE ARE FREE

from the DreamWorks film GLADIATOR

Written by HANS ZIMMER,
LISA GERRARD and KLAUS BADELT

Moderately fast

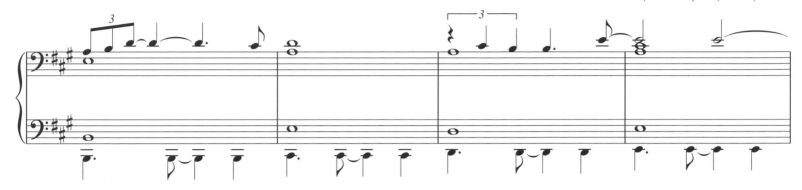

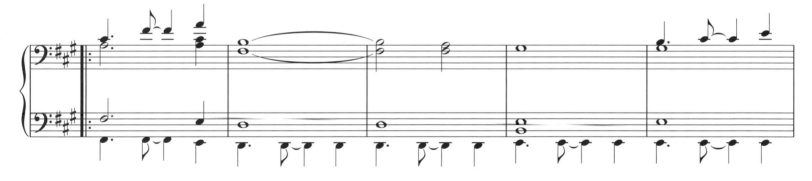

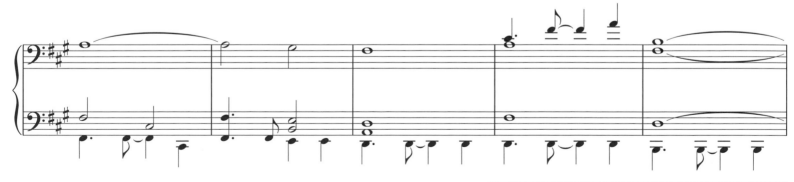

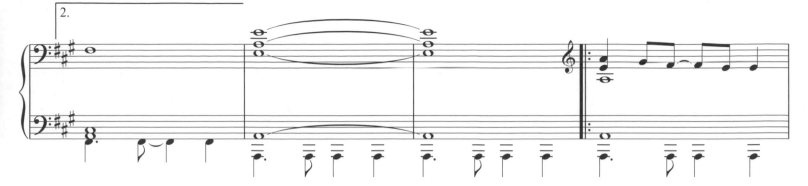

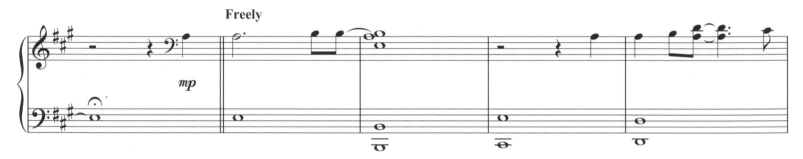

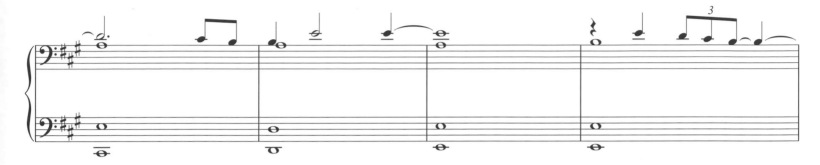

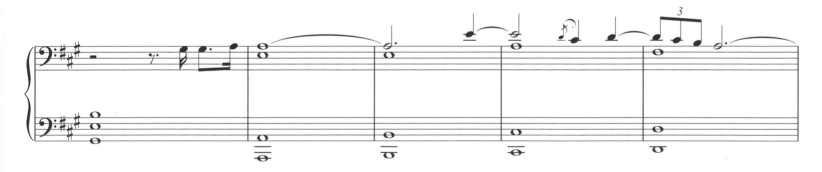

ON GOLDEN POND
Main Theme from ON GOLDEN POND

Music by DAVE GRUSIN

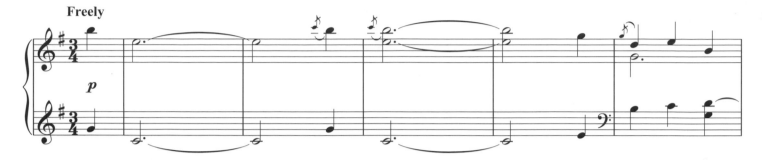

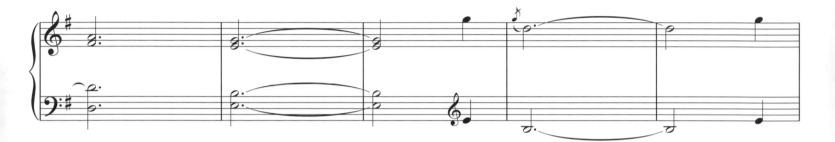

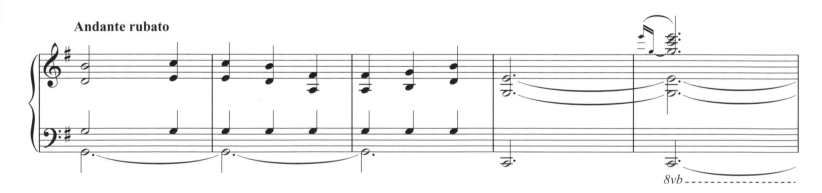

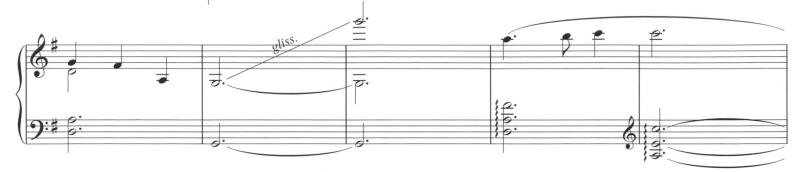

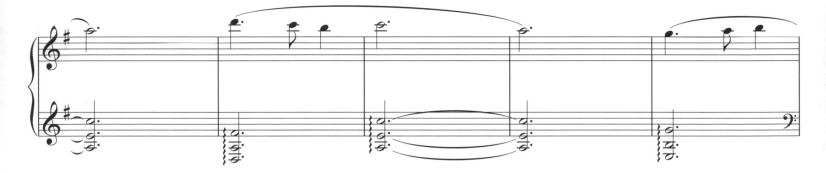

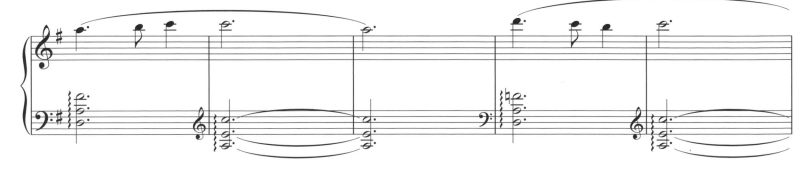

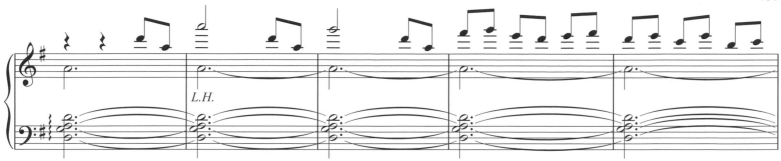

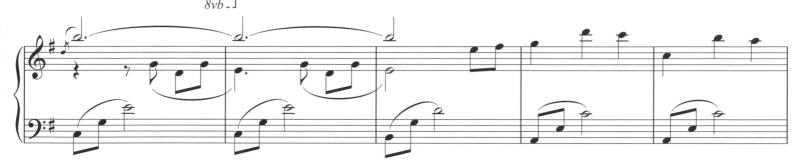

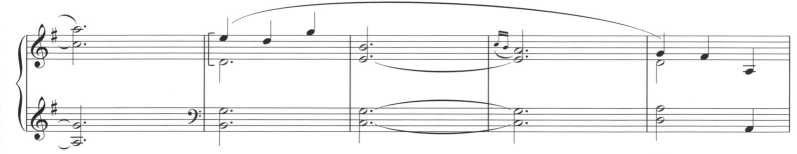

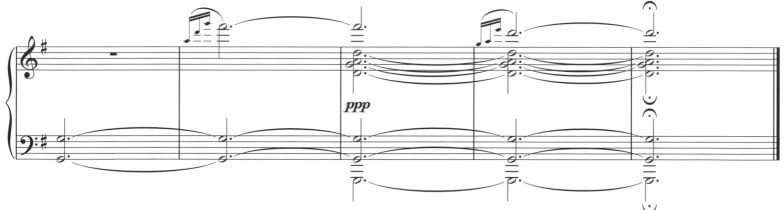

PICNIC
from the Columbia Technicolor Picture PICNIC

Words by STEVE ALLEN
Music by GEORGE W. DUNING

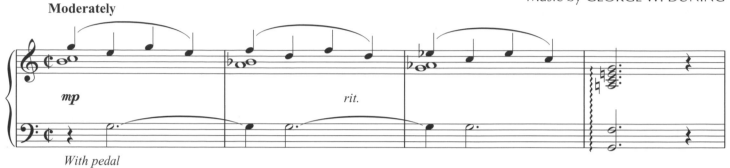

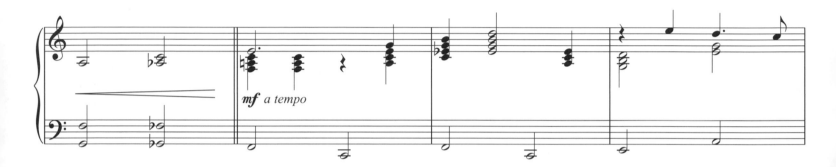

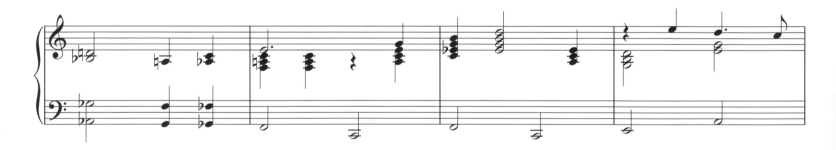

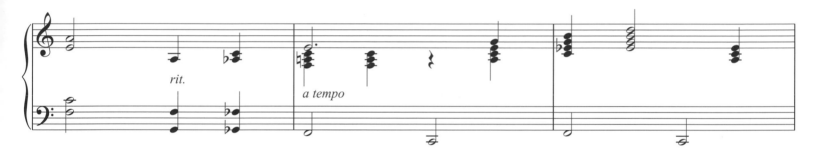

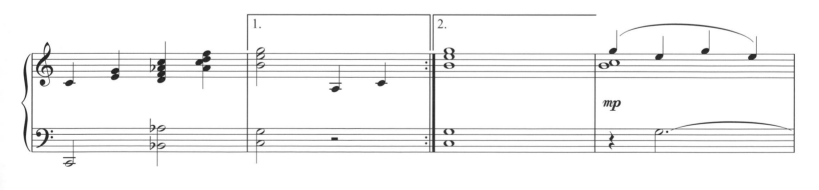

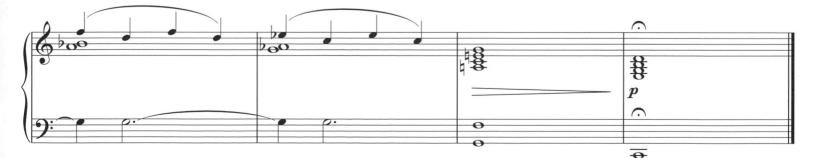

A PRAYER FOR PEACE

from MUNICH

Music by JOHN WILLIAMS

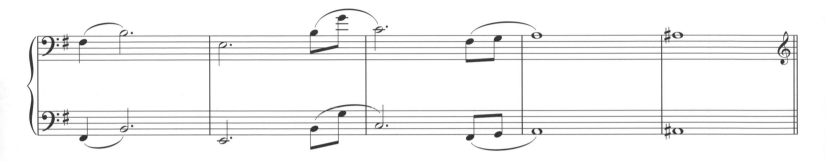

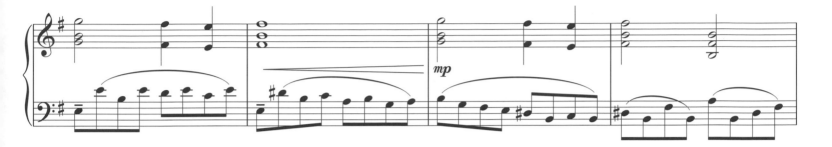

198

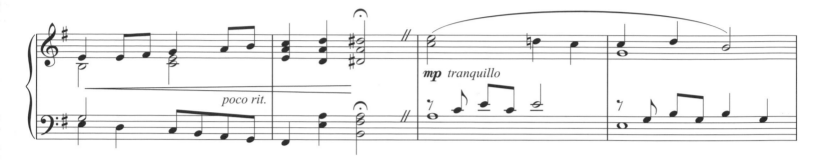

D.S. al Coda

CODA

Slower

THE PROMISE
(I'll Never Say Goodbye)
Theme from the Universal Picture THE PROMISE

Words by ALAN and MARILYN BERGMAN
Music by DAVID SHIRE

Freely, with much feeling

With pedal

Moderately

RAIDERS MARCH

from the Paramount Motion Picture RAIDERS OF THE LOST ARK

Music by JOHN WILLIAMS

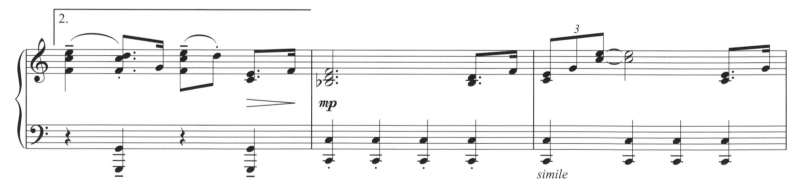

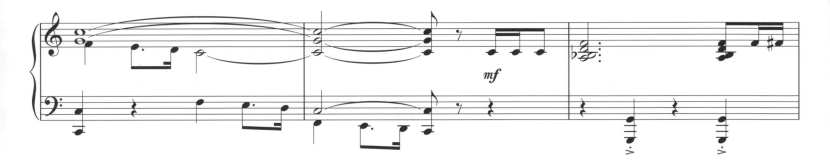

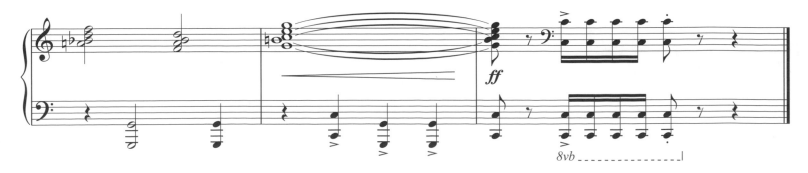

REMEMBERING EMILIE, AND FINALE

from the Motion Picture WAR HORSE

Composed by
JOHN WILLIAMS

Moderately, expressively

With pedal

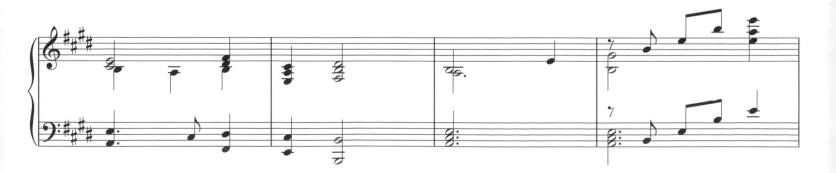

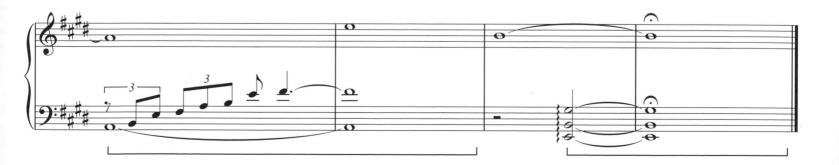

RATATOUILLE MAIN THEME

from Walt Disney Pictures' RATATOUILLE – A Pixar Film

Music by MICHAEL GIACCHINO

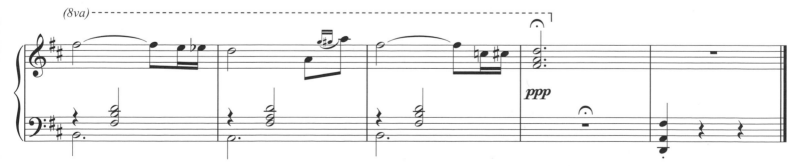

RIVER
from the Motion Picture THE MISSION

Music by ENNIO MORRICONE

no - stra vi - res no - stra poe - na no - stra sic cla - mant.

I - ra, i - ra no - stra fi - des no - stra i - ra no - stra sic cla - mant.

Vi - ta, vi - ta no - stra tel - lus no - stra vi - ta no - stra

sic cla - mant. Vi - ta, vi - ta no - stra tel - lus no - stra vi - ta

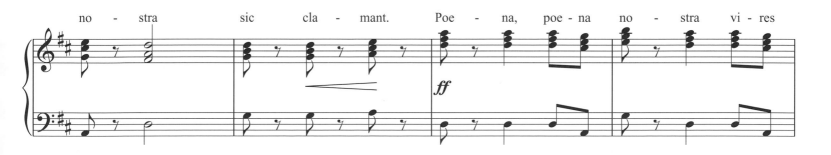

no - stra sic cla - mant. Poe - na, poe - na no - stra vi - res

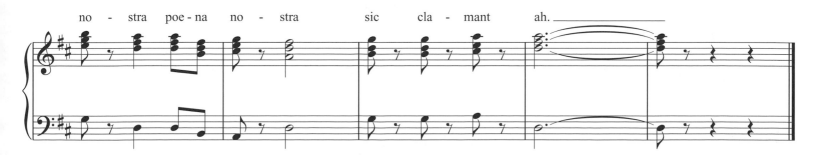

no - stra poe - na no - stra sic cla - mant ah.

RIVERSIDE WALK

from WHILE YOU WERE SLEEPING

Music by RANDY EDELMAN

𝄋 Double time (brightly)

(♪ = ♪)

To Coda ⊕ | 1.

2. | **Tempo I**

(♩ = ♪)

_mf_

_mp_

D.S. al Coda
(take repeat)

CODA

Tempo I

$(\quarternote = \eighthnote)$

1.

2.

Tempo II

$(\eighthnote = \quarternote)$

mf

mp

Tempo I

$(\quarternote = \eighthnote)$

p

ROAD TO PERDITION
from the Motion Picture ROAD TO PERDITION

By THOMAS NEWMAN

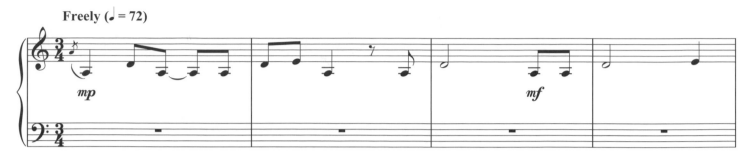

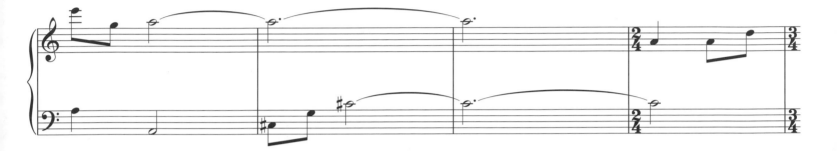

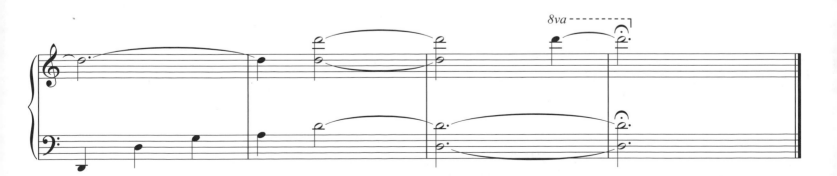

THEME FROM "SABRINA"

from the Paramount Motion Picture SABRINA

By JOHN WILLIAMS

Dreamily

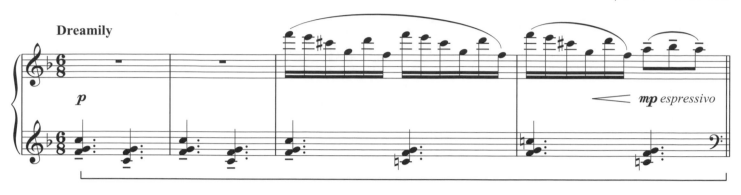

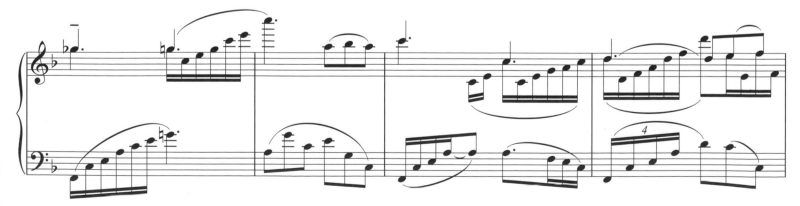

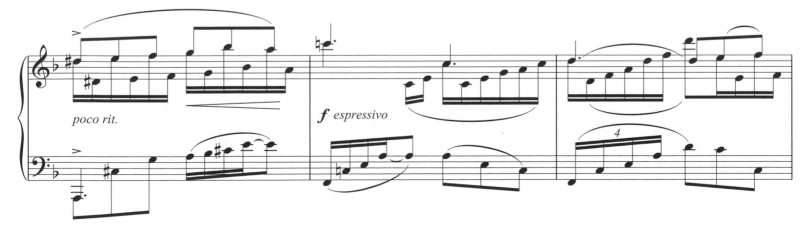

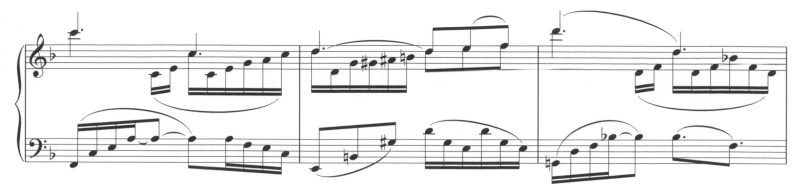

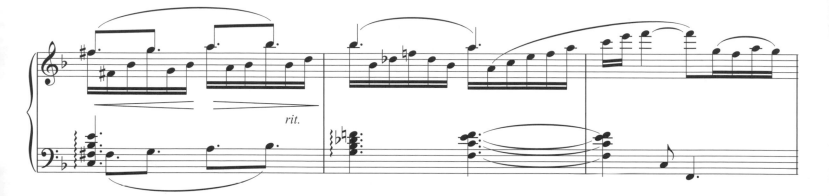

Tempo I

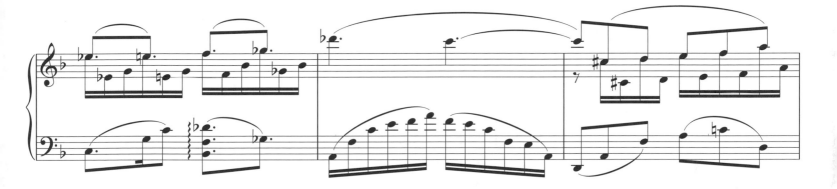

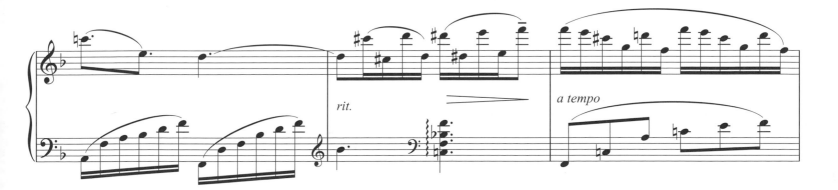

SAYURI'S THEME
from MEMOIRS OF A GEISHA

By JOHN WILLIAMS

Moderately slow, in 2

pp

With pedal

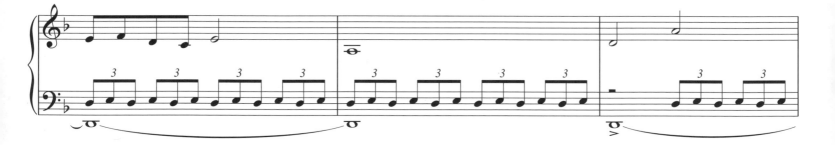

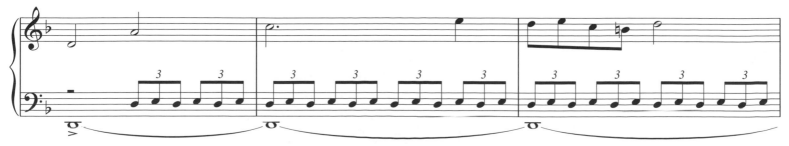

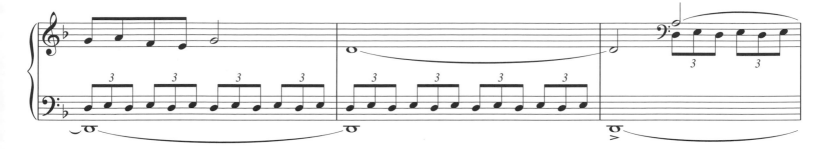

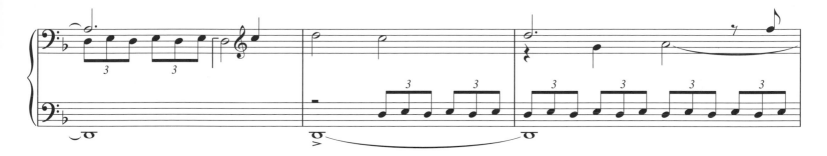

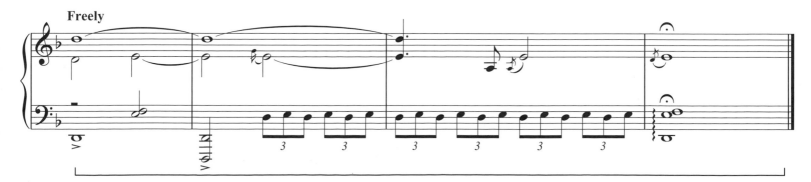

THEME FROM "SCHINDLER'S LIST"

from the Universal Motion Picture SCHINDLER'S LIST

Music by JOHN WILLIAMS

THE SEDUCTION
(Love Theme)
from the Paramount Motion Picture AMERICAN GIGOLO

Music by GIORGIO MORODER

Slowly, with a beat

To Coda ⊕

227

D.S. al Coda

CODA

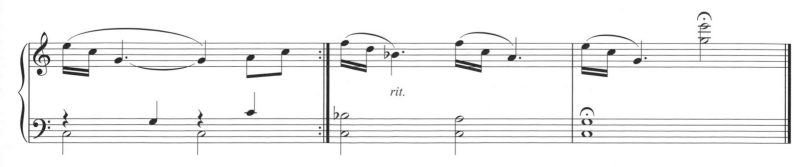

SOMEWHERE IN TIME
from SOMEWHERE IN TIME

Music by JOHN BARRY

Moderately

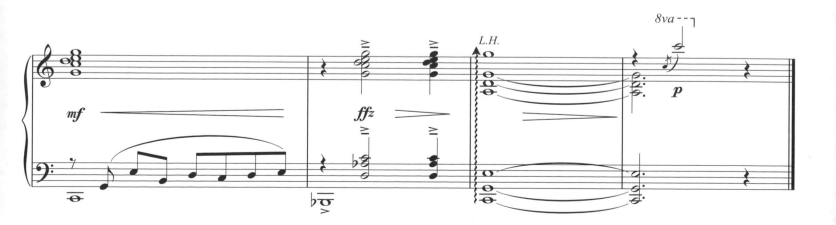

SPARTACUS – LOVE THEME

from the Universal - International Picture Release SPARTACUS

By ALEX NORTH

Moderately

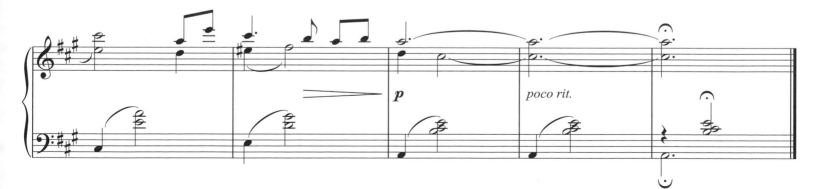

STAR WARS
(Main Theme)
from STAR WARS

Music by JOHN WILLIAMS

Majestically, steady March (♩ = 108)

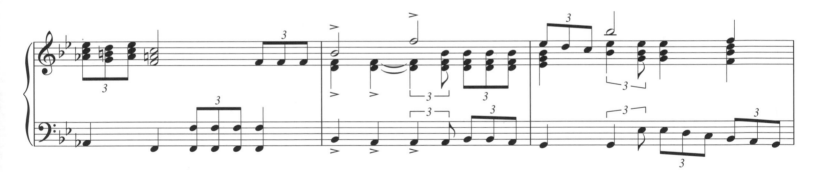

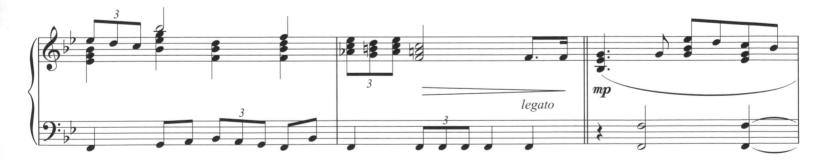

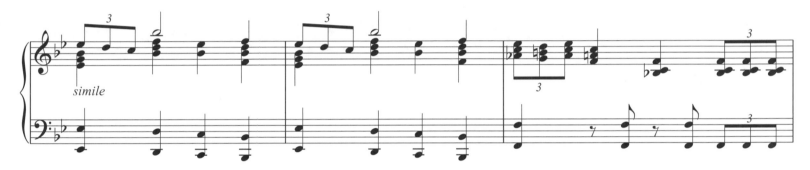

simile

simile

(Theme from)
A SUMMER PLACE
from A SUMMER PLACE

Words by MACK DISCANT
Music by MAX STEINER

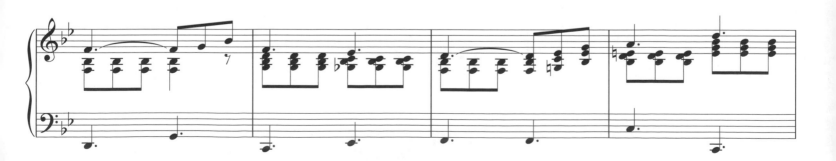

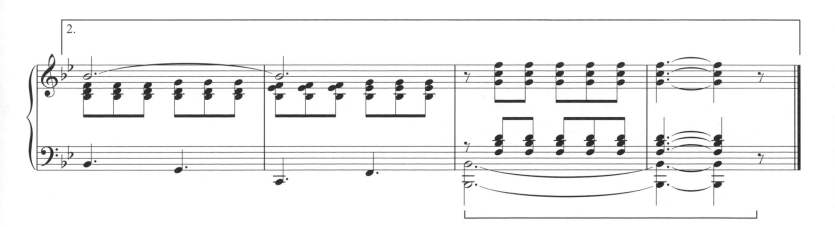

THEME FROM SUMMER OF '42
(The Summer Knows)
Theme from SUMMER OF '42

Music by MICHEL LEGRAND

Slowly

THEME FROM
"TERMS OF ENDEARMENT"

from the Paramount Picture TERMS OF ENDEARMENT

By MICHAEL GORE

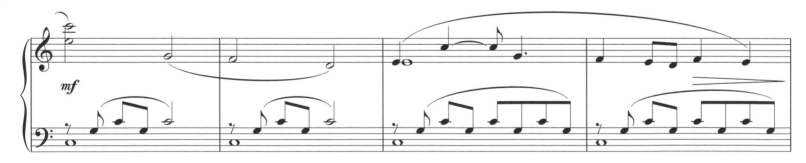

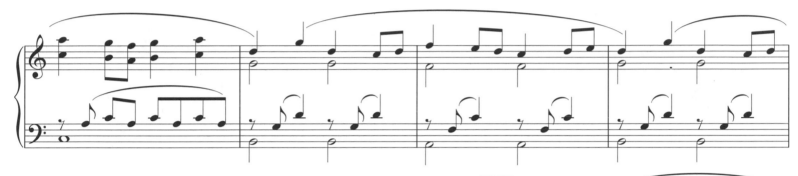

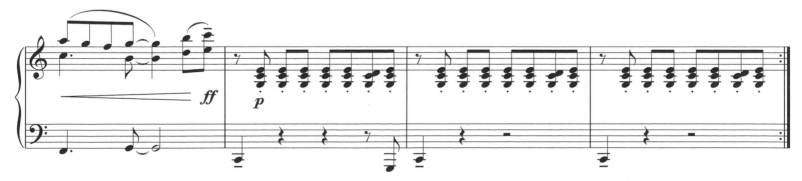

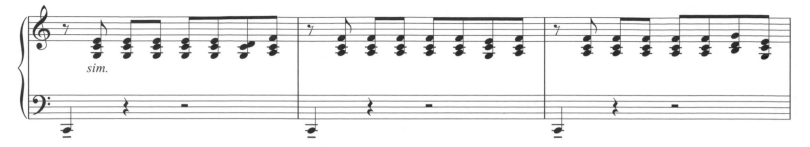

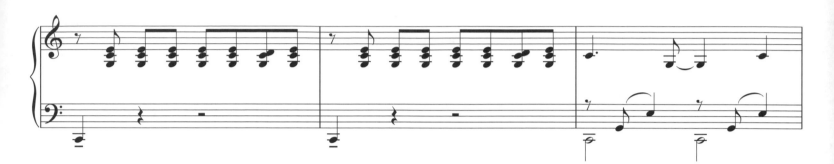

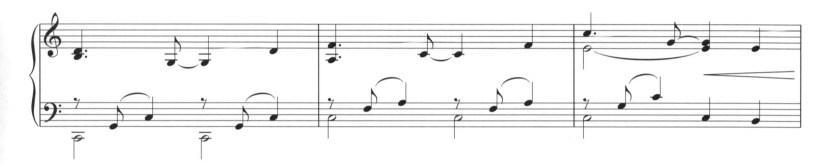

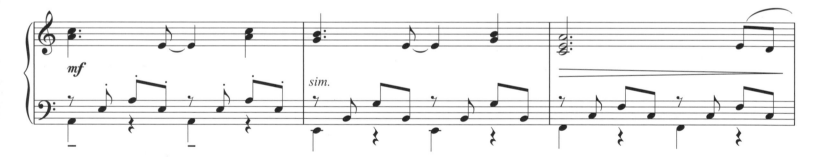

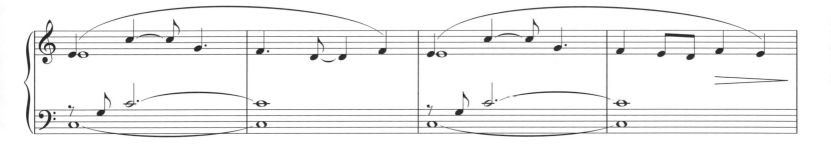

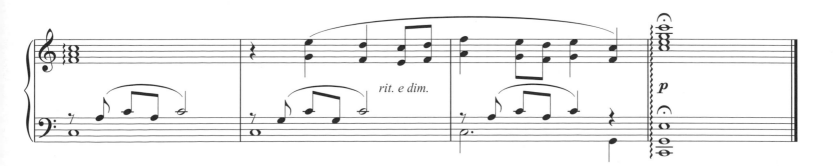

TUBULAR BELLS
Theme from THE EXORCIST

By MIKE OLDFIELD

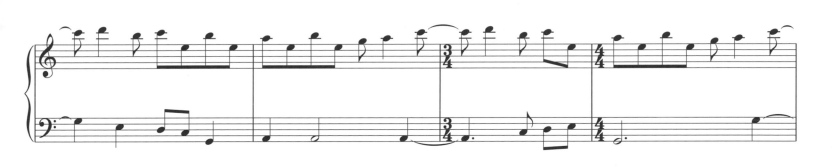

To Coda ⊕

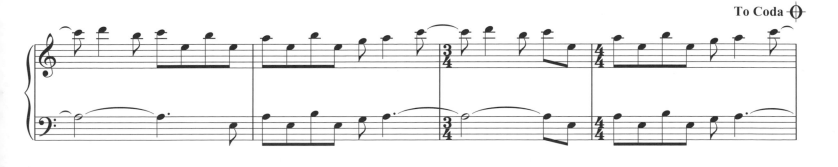

D.S. al Coda

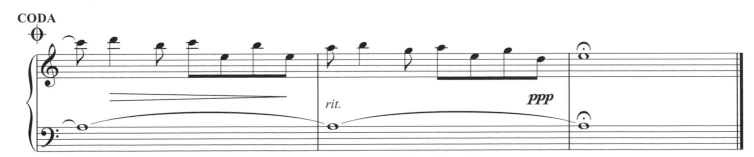

WALTZ FOR PEPPY
from the Motion Picture THE ARTIST

Composed by LUDOVIC BOURCE

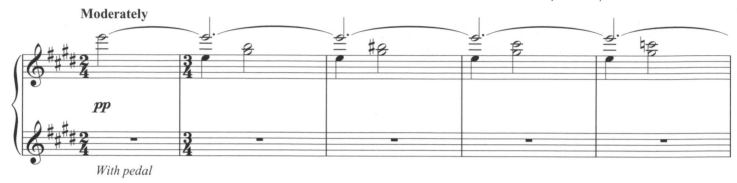

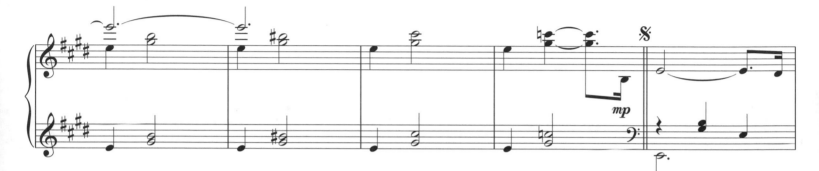

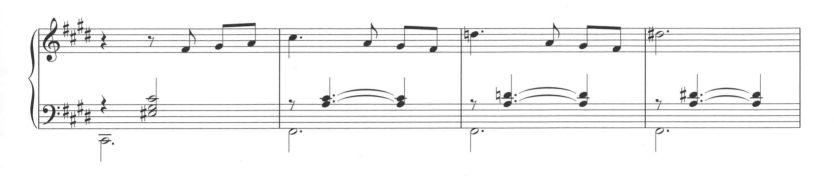

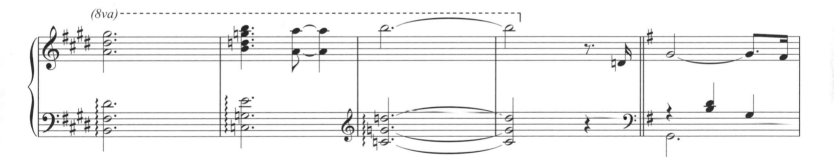

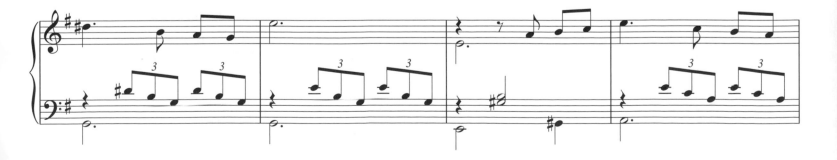

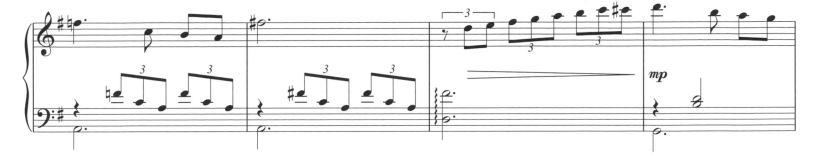

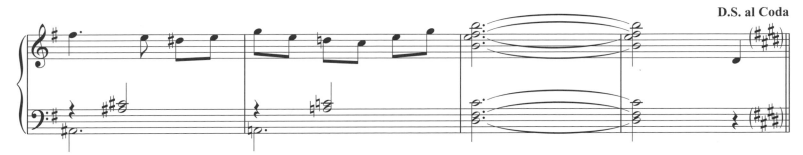

D.S. al Coda

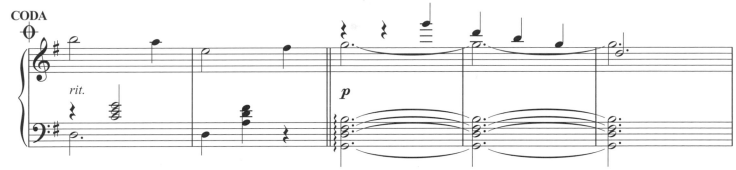

Slowly, with freedom

CODA

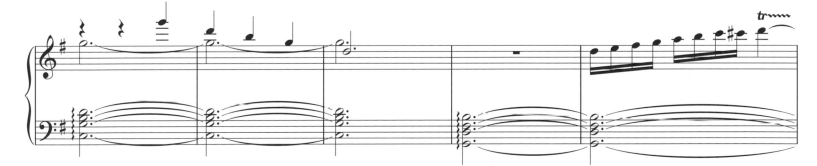

THE WINGS
from BROKEBACK MOUNTAIN

By GUSTAVO SANTAOLALLA

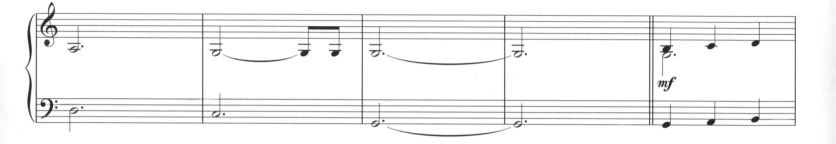

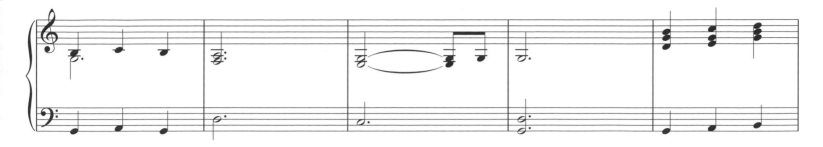

TEST DRIVE
from the Motion Picture HOW TO TRAIN YOUR DRAGON

By JOHN POWELL

Moderately

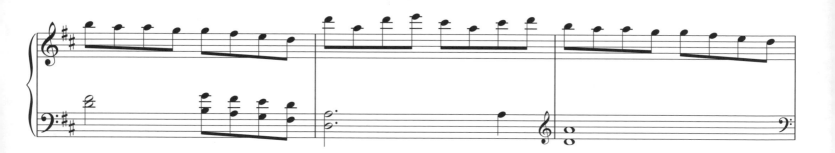

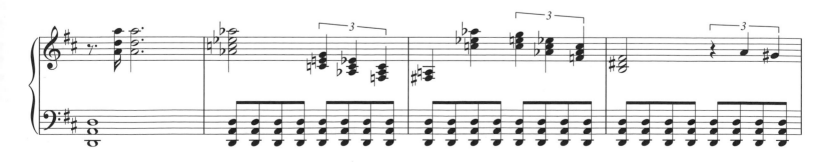

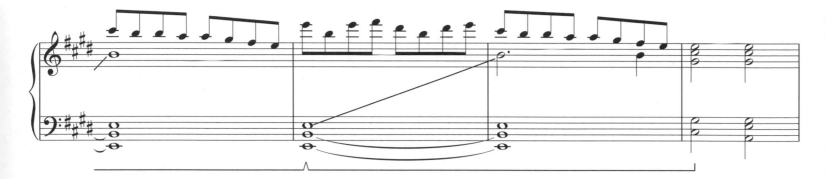